Pragmatic™
ENTERPRISE ARCHITECTURE
CONNECTING THE DOTS™
www.PragmaticEA.com

Enterprise Transformation Culture

The Inconvenient Pragmatic Truth

AF895570

v2021

Kevin Lee Smith

First published: 1 July 2017
Last updated: January 2021

ISBN 978-1-908424-60-0 (hardback)
ISBN 978-1-908424-59-4 (paperback)
ISBN 978-1-908424-61-7 (ebook)

Published by:
Pragmatic365 Ltd
25 Buttermere
Great Notley,
Essex CM77 7UY
England

www.Pragmatic365.org

Currently Available Reference Books	ISBN	Pre-requisites
The Pragmatic Family of Frameworks A **Pragmatic** Introduction	978-1-908424-42-6	
Enterprise Fundamentals A **Pragmatic** Approach Using PEFF	978-1-908424-42-6	
Enterprise Transformation A **Pragmatic** Approach using POET	978-1-908424-07-5	PEFF
Enterprise Architecture A **Pragmatic** Approach using PEAF	978-1-908424-10-5	POET

Currently Available Focus Books	ISBN	Pre-requisites
PEAF 4 TOGAF Kick-start Your TOGAF Adoption. **Pragmatically**	978-1-908424-25-9	
Transformation Governance A **Pragmatic** Approach using Transformation Debt™	978-1-908424-48-8	
Enterprise Architecture Tools A **Pragmatic** Approach to EA Tool Selection and Adoption	978-1-908424-54-9	
What is EA A **Pragmatic** Explanation	978-1-908424-57-0	
Transformation Culture The Inconvenient **Pragmatic** Truth	978-1-908424-59-4	
Transformation Maturity Assessment A **Pragmatic** Approach using the PTMC	978-1-908424-63-1	
Connecting the DOTS™ The Death of "The Business" & "IT"	978-1-908424-68-6	

Coming Soon	ISBN	Pre-requisites
Enterprise Direction A **Pragmatic** Approach using POED	978-1-908424-16-7	PEFF
Enterprise Operation A **Pragmatic** Approach using POEO	978-1-908424-19-8	PEFF
Enterprise Support A **Pragmatic** Approach using POES	978-1-908424-22-8	PEFF
Enterprise Engineering A **Pragmatic** Approach using PEEF	978-1-908424-13-6	POET

This work was inspired by all those who seek to make the world a better place, rather than those who seek to own it.

"We cannot solve our problems,
with the same thinking we used when we created them."

Albert Einstein

"Sometimes it is the people who no one imagines anything of,
who do the things that no one can imagine."

Alan Turing

"Computers are useless.
They can only give you answers"

Pablo Picasso.

"You cannot 'cost justify' Architecture"

J. A. Zachman

"We have seen the enemy,
and the enemy is us (management)."

W. E. Deming

"If I have seen further,
it is by standing on the shoulders of giants."

Isaac Newton

Acknowledgements

The author would like to acknowledge the extensive help and advice provided by Murphy to get this book to market, particularly for the constant companionship and irritating interruptions (which provided much needed relief although I didn't know it at the time) and a chance for mutual tummy tickles.

I would also like to thank my wife, Virginia, for her moral support and the constant supply of Marmite on toast.

Please note that, to preserve commercial and personal confidentiality, any stories and examples in this book will usually have been adapted, combined and in part fictionalised from experiences in a variety of contexts, and do not and are not intended to represent any specific individual or Enterprise.

PEAF CONTRIBUTOR

Pragmatic thanks the following people who have contributed their ideas.

(In country alphabetical order)

If you would like to contribute ideas or have any comments or suggestions for improvements or corrections, please **contact us**.

Australia

Hungary

New Zealand

United Kingdom

United Kingdom

United Kingdom

United States

United States

Zimbabwe

Contributor		Area of Contributions
	**Taiss Quartapa** Interim Executive Enlightened Interest Group **Australia**	Exploring the impossible is my calling. Whether that means working on the Enterprise Architecture, reinventing the internal processes of a global company or creating a new, innovative approach for the retail experience, solving the impossible is what I seek to do. I'm driven to deliver impactful results which enhance aspects of people's lives. **POET > Culture > Slaves-to-Psychology > The-Dunning-Kruger-Effect**
	**Tamás Nacsák** Senior Enterprise Architect Telcotrend **Hungary**	Tamás Nacsák, is a Senior Enterprise Architect, worked twenty plus years in IT mostly in the telecommunication industry; the last twelve dedicated to Enterprise Architecture. He is currently working as Enterprise Architect on several Telco companies and at Hungarian State Tresury. **POET > Culture > The-Architect > The-Pragmatic-Architect-Creed**
	**Brendan S. McEnroe** Chief Technology Officer // Enterprise Architect Trade Window Limited **New Zealand**	Brendan is a Certified Enterprise Architect, technology thought leader and start-up founder with 30 years' experience. He has a demonstrated history of digital strategy, innovation and leading high performing teams on large scale technology projects, across UK and NZ organisations. **PEFF > Adoption > Measures > PTMC > Tools**
	**Gareth Llewellyn** Enterprise and Solution Architect Freelance **United Kingdom**	Over 28 years, Gareth has been a trusted advisor to executives and key decision makers. He has architected strategic transformations for medium to large commercial organisations, and to federal, state and local government across the UK and Australia. Gareth uses design thinking to transition businesses to their target operating model, delivering profound outcomes while reducing cost & risk. **POET > Culture > The-Architect > What-Does-An-Architect-Do**
	**Amber Smith** Trainee Cabinetmaker Humphrey Munson **United Kingdom**	As someone who likes to learn, and loves a challenge, I have tried working in many different industries, some of which I loved, some I absolutely hated. I have come to know myself through trying new things. Recently, I have attained a job which I absolutely love, and aspire to turn into my career. Cabinetmaking allows me to be practical, creative, and keeps me on my toes! **POET > Culture > Slaves-to-Psychology > The-Dunning-Kruger-Effect**
	**Abdul Aziz** Business Architect and Cybernetician Vanga Limited **United Kingdom**	A passionate strategist, enterprise architect and business change leader endeavouring to help executives, managers and operatives navigate complexity with principles and values that enable their organisational purpose. Abdul has over 20 years' experience in all aspects of "changing the business" across multiple industries holds an MBA with distinction from the Alliance Manchester Business School. **POET > Culture > Architecture-and-Engineering > Fundamentals**

James McGovern
Research Director
Gartner
United States

Over twenty years of experience applying technical, process, and people skills to improve individual, team, and organizational performance and overall efficacy. Advanced knowledge of enterprise architecture and enterprise security with a focus on high-profile customer-facing applications. An impassioned leader who mentors with purpose and understands that strong working relationships create great

PEAF > Culture > Roles > EASG-Enterprise-Architecture-Steering-Group

Pedro M. Correa
Harbinger of things to come
Papyrus Software
United States

Regional IT industry leader with SMET background and 25+ years of international experience in the Americas. Award winner for: leading regional sales and service delivery CoE while working as CTO (EDS), for Regional LATAM Sales/Marketing Director (Texas Instruments) and for Business Analyst/PMP (IBM)

PEAF > Methods > Phases > Roadmapping > Intermediate-Journey

Murambwa Clever Haparari
Technology Lead and Design Authority
FBC Holdings
Zimbabwe

Technology Innovation and Enterprise Architecture Leader with a vision to become an Enterprise Transformation leader driving Enterprises for the consistent achievement of their Strategic goals of Effectiveness, Efficiency, Agility and Sustainability of both the Operations and Transformation capabilities through appropriate adoption of the Enterprise Architecture Paradigm.

PEAF > Artefacts > Meta-models > Structural

Contents

FOREWORD

Why Should I Read This Book?

Enterprises (Public Companies, Private Companies, Government Agencies) spend a lot of money on Transformation initiatives, and in trying to mature how they plan and execute those initiatives. A lot of time and money is spent on processes and IT tools to help an Enterprise plan and run projects better. However, after all this time and money is spent, processes are changed, new tools are bought and installed, still the overall numbers are that 70% of all projects fail. How can this be? The simple answer is that the culture at large in most Enterprise Transformation capabilities (the unwritten rules and regulations) are perfectly engineered to produce a 70% failure rate. So put away your tools, and start thinking about culture today.

Culture trumps Everything™ is much much more than just a saying. It is a very cold hard fact, which if ignored, literally has the capacity to destroy civilisations.

Who Should Read This Book?

Anyone and everyone that is involved (in whole or in part) in the Transformation of Enterprises, from CxO's and Directors to Database Support technicians. From Project Managers to Business Analysts. From Management Consultants to Programmers, and any one of a thousand other job titles that are (in whole or in part) concerned with the Transformation of Enterprises.

Why Should I attend a Workshop?

Run over 1 day and using this book, the workshop exposes the culture that exists in many enterprises. It gets the attendees thinking in terms of culture, different ways to think about it, the role psychology plays, how the two tribes of "the business" and "IT" contrast, and over 40 keypoints to help focus the mind.

Your Enterprise is already spending a lot of money on Transformation initiatives, and so it is imperative that your Enterprise stands the best chance of reducing the 70% failure rate.

This Workshop will provide you with the context and approach to give you that best chance of success.

PF2™

Pragmatic Family of Frameworks

Pragmatic 365
CONNECTING THE DOTS

The **Pragmatic Family of Frameworks (PF2)** is defined by its Mission Statement:

> "To provide Enterprises with **Pragmatic** frameworks to enable them to increase their maturity in how they fulfil their Mission"

This introduction to the **PF2** sets out the companies involved, the Licensing terms and what Training there is available. It also set out what frameworks are part of **PF2**, how they relate to each other, and how they relate to other frameworks,

KEYPOINT:

PF2 introduces the Companies and Frameworks that are part of the Pragmatic Family.

ADOPTION:

Management: Instigate a project to ensure everyone related to Transformation is trained in Pragmatic's Family of Frameworks.

Questions to Ponder

- What Frameworks does your Enterprise Use?

Introduction

> KEYPOINT:
>
> The Introduction section of PF2 introduces the companies that are part of the Pragmatic Family.

Questions to Ponder

- Do you think fundamental terminology is useful to your Enterprise?
- What fundamental terminology does your Enterprise use?
- If none, what fundamental terminology do you think would be appropriate?

Introduction > Companies

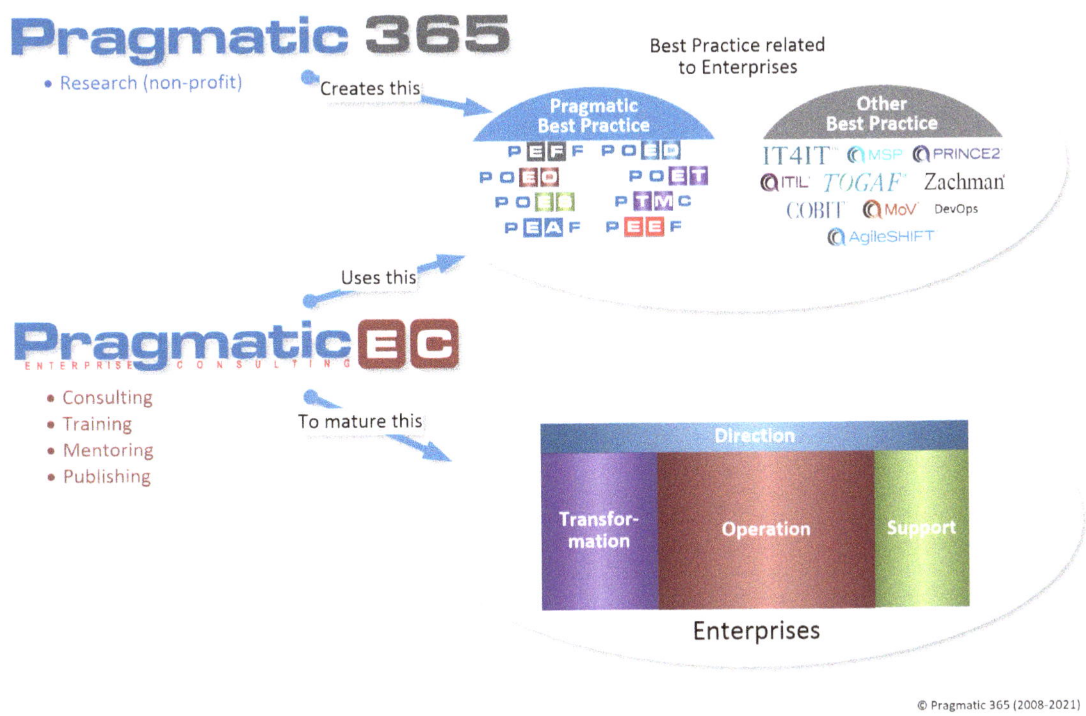

Pragmatic 365 is a non-profit research company (hereinafter referred to as **Pragmatic**) dedicated to developing Best Practice in relation to the structure and transformation of Enterprises. All profits are poured back into the continuous evolution and creation of best practice. This best practice, contributes to the existing best practice in the marketplace, such as PRINCE2, MSP, TOGAF, etc. Pragmatic is tracking over 900 frameworks currently in the marketplace.

Pragmatic EC is a consulting company which uses any appropriate Best Practice (whether developed by **Pragmatic** or not) to help Enterprises mature any or all parts of their Transformation Capability (from Strategy to Deployment). This is done by consulting, training, mentoring and publishing.

Pragmatic EC is unique, because it's domain of excellence is, **HOW** Enterprises effect Transformation not the doing Transformation. That is, our mission is to help Enterprises mature their Transformation capability, not their Operations capability. This contrasts with almost all other consultancies, which concentrate on improving the Operations part of Enterprises, and as such have people who are experts in various business verticals such as Financial, Pharma, Energy, Health, etc.

Pragmatic EC can work with Enterprises in any business vertical, since the fundamentals of an Enterprises Transformation capability, is not dependant upon the type of Business they are in. The way that HR or Finance is carried out, is fundamentally the same in all Enterprises. So, the way Transformation is carried out (or rather should be carried out) is the same in all Enterprises. The output of HR, Finance and Transformation may be directed towards a specific business vertical, but the fundamentals of HR, Finance and Transformation are the same for all.

Our centre of excellence is therefore...

The Transformation of Transformation.

> KEYPOINT:
>
> Pragmatic 365 is a non-profit research company. Pragmatic EC is a consulting company.

> ADOPTION:
>
> Management: Engage Pragmatic EC to assess and help you to mature your Enterprise's Transformation capability.

Questions to Ponder

- What Companies do you know of, that create best practice relating to Enterprise Transformation?
- What Consultancies do you know of, that are focussed on the Transformation of Transformation, rather than the Transformation of Operations?

Introduction > Companies > Pragmatic EC

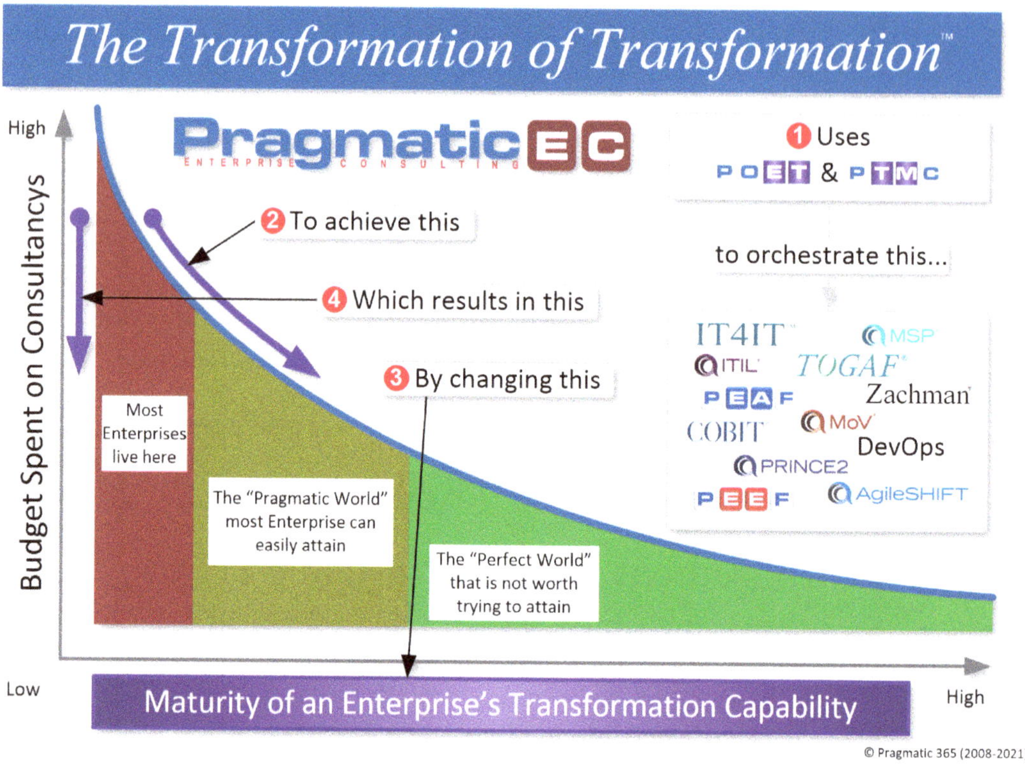

Most consultancies won't tell you what **Pragmatic** will tell you.

Most consultancy's revenue streams, are **inversely** proportional to how mature their client's Transformation Capability is. Most consultancies are therefore motivated, NOT to mature an Enterprise's Transformation Capability. The more immature an Enterprise's Transformation Capability is, the more money the consultancy is likely to make, in fixing all the problems that will arise. Have you ever wondered why the "70% of all project fail" statistic hasn't changed for 40 years? Now you know!

Because most Enterprises primary function and expertise is NOT in relation to Transformation, they tend to live in the Red area depicted on the graph. Their Transformation capabilities are barely mature enough to effect the transformation they require, and the result is missed deadlines, blown budgets, unfulfilled customer expectations, and as a result, large consultancy bills.

The green area illustrates a "perfect world" where the Enterprise is supremely mature in its Transformation capability. There is little reason to try to attain such levels of maturity as the law of diminishing returns applies.

The yellow area indicates the sweet spot, where the level of maturity is both appropriate and attainable.

Pragmatic is different from almost all other consultancies. We concentrate on enabling Enterprises to move from the Red area to the Yellow area. This is achieved by:

1) Utilising POET and the PTMC to orchestrate Best Practice…
2) To move an Enterprise's Transformation capability from the red to the yellow…
3) Which is accomplished by increasing the maturity of an Enterprises Transformation capability…
4) Which results in a large decrease in the time and money spent on Consultancies.

We believe that anything that can be done to reduce an Enterprise's reliance on external consultancies (and their associated costs and risks) is a good thing.

Pragmatic's Mission is…

> "To provide Enterprises with **Pragmatic** frameworks to enable them to increase their maturity in HOW they effect Transformation/Change"

Pragmatic's Vision is…

> "The Transformation of Transformation. "

KEYPOINT:

Most consultancies only want to sell you fish.

Pragmatic will teach you how to fish.

ADOPTION:

Management: Engage Pragmatic EC to help you reign in the budget spent on consultancies and therefore Transformation.

Questions to Ponder

- Which consultancies do you know of, which help you improve HOW you do Transformation vs those that just want to help you DO Transformation?
- How much could you reduce your annual Transformation budget by, if you matured HOW you do Transformation?

Pragmatic NON-COMMERCIAL LICENSE

- ✓ 350 Companies
- ✓ 130 Government Bodies
- ✓ 60 Academic Institutions
- ✓ 3,700 Individuals

Pragmatic COMMERCIAL LICENSE

- ✓ 43 Consultancies
- ✓ 13 Training Providers
- ✓ 11 Tool Vendors

As at Q1/2021

Non-Commercial (Internal)

If you wish to use any of **Pragmatic**'s Ontologies, Frameworks or materials (in whole or in part) internally, that is, to improve the Transformation Capability of your Enterprise, then your Enterprise, and the people that use them, only require a Non-Commercial License.

The **Pragmatic** Non-Commercial license is issued FREE and is automatically renewed for FREE on an annual basis.

The license is issued with the following terms:

- Any use must be attributable to **Pragmatic 365**.
- Details of the license issued will be posted on the **Pragmatic 365** website.
- **Pragmatic's** Ontologies, Frameworks or materials cannot be used for profit externally.
- The Licensee is entitled to use the Licensee Logo on promotional materials.
- When used on a website the logo must link back to www.Pragmatic365.org
- Licensees agree to be contacted by **Pragmatic 365** periodically with updates.

Applications for a license can be made at http://www.Pragmatic365.org/licensing-non-commercial.asp

Commercial (External)

If you wish to use any of **Pragmatic's** Ontologies, Frameworks or materials (in whole or in part) externally, that is, to improve the Transformation Capability of your clients Enterprises (not your own) (e.g. Consultancies, Training Providers and Tool Vendors), then your Enterprise, and the people that use them, must possess a Commercial License.

> **NOTE:** Contractors who operate their own one-man-band companies and provide services through recruitment agencies to End-User Organisations and Government Bodies are not considered to be consultancies and therefore only require a Non-Commercial License.

If you wish to evaluate any of **Pragmatic's** Ontologies, Frameworks or materials internally for commercial use, you can do so under a free Non-Commercial License.

If you wish to evaluate any of **Pragmatic's** Ontologies, Frameworks or materials for external commercial use (by using it with an external client) this is possible by contacting **Pragmatic** first and obtaining written permission to do so.

The license is issued with the following terms:

- Any use must be attributable to **Pragmatic 365**.
- Details of the license issued will be posted on the **Pragmatic 365** website.
- **Pragmatic's** Ontologies, Frameworks or materials can be used for profit externally.
- The Licensee is entitled to use the Licensee Logo on their websites and other promotional materials.
- When used on a website the logo must link back to www.Pragmatic365.org
- Licensees agree to be contacted by **Pragmatic 365** periodically with updates.
- It is expressly forbidden to pass on any **Pragmatic** Commercial Licensing Fees to clients of the commercial Enterprise, either directly or indirectly.
- The Standard Commercial License specifically prohibits the production of derivative frameworks, however, if you wish to create derivative frameworks this is possible by contacting **Pragmatic 365** and obtaining explicit written consent.

To apply for a license, please see http://www.Pragmatic365.org/licensing-commercial.asp

KEYPOINT:

Use Pragmatic Frameworks (for free) to improve your Enterprise.

ADOPTION:

Management: Apply for a Pragmatic Commercial or Non-Commercial license depending on your circumstances.

Questions to Ponder

- Which License is best for you?

Introduction > Training > Certification Courses

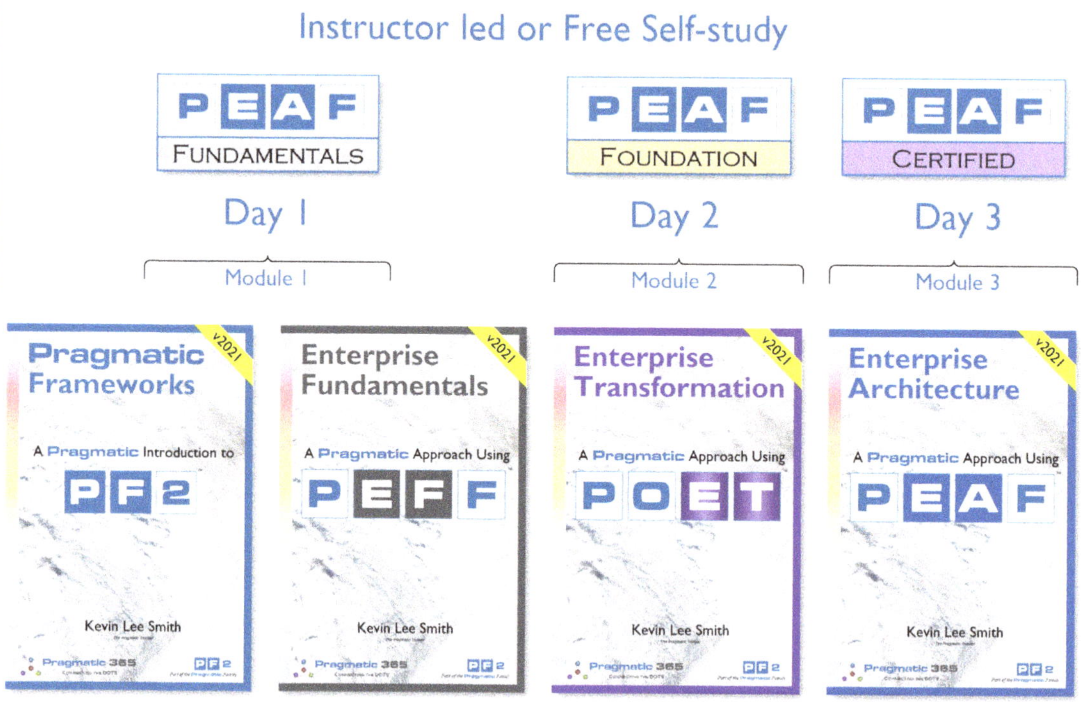

© Pragmatic 365 (2008-2021)

There are three levels which build toward PEAF Certified status. PEAF Fundamentals training is a pre-requisite for PEAF Foundation training is a pre-requisite for PEAF Certified training, because PEAF inherits and builds on the **Pragmatic** Operating model for Enterprise Transformation defined by POET which in turn inherits and builds on the **Pragmatic** Enterprise Fundamentals Framework.

These courses educate individuals and Enterprises in a vendor and technology neutral **Pragmatic** approach to improving their Transformation capability in general and the Enterprise Architecture part of that domain, in particular.

You can choose from Self-Study or Instructor led formats.

- **Self Study Training** is **FREE** and is split into three modules. Each module corresponds to the content taught in the classroom. You can stop and start whenever you like. To move on to the next Module, you must pass all preceding exams. How long you take to study and how often you take the exams is completely up to you. You only pay for certification exams if you want to take them.
- **Instructor led Training and Certification** is fee based, and run by a **Pragmatic 365** Certified Trainer. Each day consists of 6 hours of presentation and discussions, finishing with a 1 hour Exam.

In addition, **Pragmatic** also offers various 1 day workshops targeted at specific subject areas.

Certification Courses

- **PEAF Fundamentals** (1 day) sets out the basic language and ontologies used throughout all **Pragmatic**'s Frameworks.
- **PEAF Foundation** (1 day) sets out an Operating Model for the whole of the transformation domain (from Strategy to Deployment) and the common patterns of methods and artefacts that allow an organisation to tactically improve parts of it while preserving the effectiveness and efficiency of the whole. It sets the context for Enterprise Architecture in terms of where it fits in, and where it doesn't.
- **PEAF Certified** (1 days) concentrates on the specifics of the EA domain and sets out the fundamental pieces to be put in place to be successful.

Certification Exams

- Exams are marked dynamically in real-time, and so if you get an answer wrong or partially wrong, you will receive feedback for example "Correct but you need to give a little more detail".
- The pass mark for all exams is 100%. The reason for this is that we want to make sure that people understand 100% of the things an exam is asking (which is only a small proportion of the entire content).
- Most people complete each exam in 45-60 minutes, and although there is no hard time limit as such, we will close each exam after 2 hours.
- If you fail an exam, you are welcome to re-sit the exam (maximum of 3 times) at a later time for no additional cost

Target Audience

The course is suitable for anyone who is interested in maturing **how** Transformation and change is effected within an Enterprise and how Enterprise Architecture fits in and helps with that.

Prior Knowledge

No prior knowledge of Enterprise Architecture is required, although it is useful if the attendees have worked as part of the Transformation capability of an Enterprise.

Relevant Industries.

Learning the fundamental discipline of Enterprise Architecture (and the wider Transformation domain) and how to mature it in an Enterprise is not dependent upon any business industry knowledge.

Previous Customers

Experian, Hasbro, Freshfields Bruckhaus Deringer, California Franchise Tax Board, California Department of Health Care Services, Aspen Re, Dunn & Bradstreet, California State Board of Equalization.

Private/On Site Courses

Can be run and tailored to the challenges of your Enterprise.

Certification Body

The certificating body is **Pragmatic 365** Ltd. A Non-Profit.

Previous comments

We have a 100% positive feedback from the course. Some comments below but all comments (unedited and unabridged) can be read at www.pragmatic365.org/credibility-comments-training.asp

> "Excellent, thought provoking and well laid out"
>
> ***- Global Automation Manager, UK***

> "Energizing and invigorating -- helps put the passion back in EA efforts"
>
> ***- VP Marketing & Business Development, USA***

> "It was fantastic course - very insigthful and valuable. Thank you."
>
> ***- Architect, UK***

> "A refreshing approach to EA, focused on *helping* the business develop an approach and strategy, rather than telling them what to do. The course was very logical and easy to follow."
>
> ***- Executive Director, USA***

Do people recommend PEAF?

92% of people would recommend PEAF to others. Some comments are show below but all comments (unedited and unabridged) can be read at www.pragmatic365.org/credibility-comments-survey.asp

"I would recommend PEAF because PEAF has a down to earth holistic enterprise approach that makes EA goals and approach understandable by stakeholders, management and practitioners"

- EA, Independent EA, Greece

"I would recommend PEAF because It is a great straight forward place to start looking into EA. The concept are straightforward and both easy to apply and understand."

- ICT Architect, Australia

"I would recommend PEAF because of it's logical and Pragmatic approach to EA. I find it less academic than some of the other frameworks."

- Enterprise Solution Architect, South Africa

"I would recommend PEAF because a) Provides a good roadmap for transformation b) Vendor and technology neutral c) Simplifies the EA artefacts d) Most comprehensive framework"

- Consultant, India

KEYPOINT:

PEAF Certified training, provides everything to enable you to adopt PEAF.

ADOPTION:

Management: Engage Pragmatic EC to deliver PEAF Certified Transformation Best Practice training.

Questions to Ponder

- Have you read any of these books?
- If so, what did you like? What did you not like?
- Have you been on any of these courses?
- If so, what did you like? What did you not like?
- Which course would interest you the most?

Introduction > Training > Focused Workshops

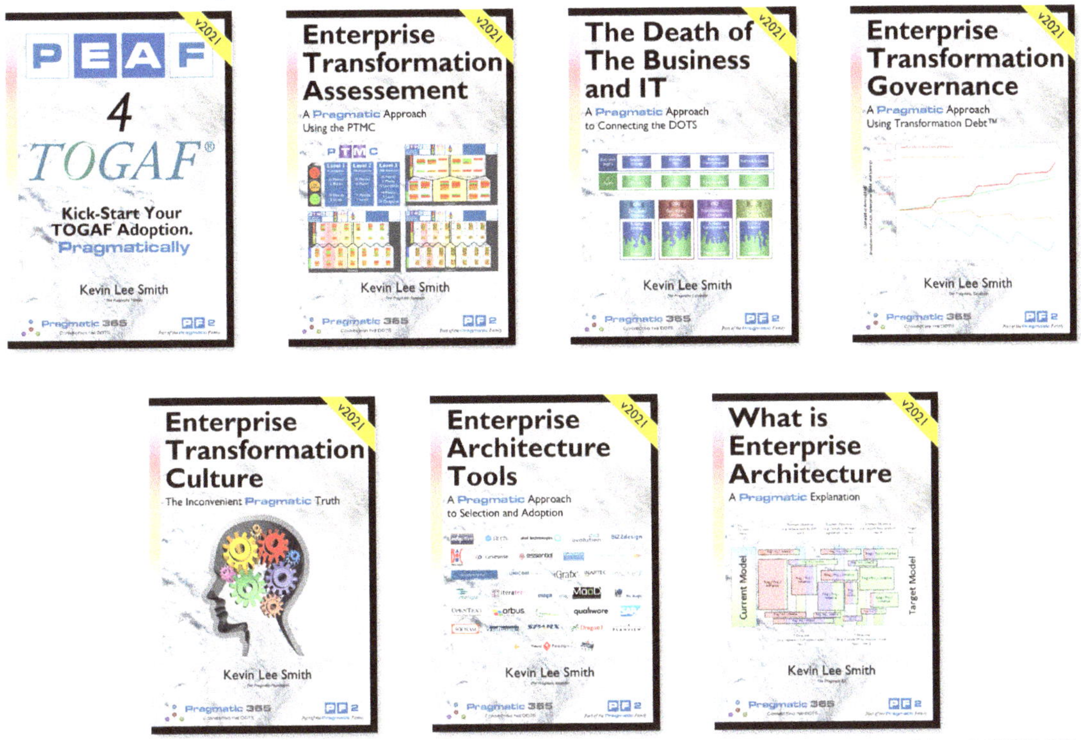

Various workshops are available based on specially selected content from the base PEFF/POET/PEAF material, which focuses on particular areas of concern.

You can choose from Self-Study or Instructor led formats.

- **Self Study Training** is **FREE** although obviously does not provide people with the workshop type of environment that allows for specific issues to be discussed. However, Self Studying this content does work towards your PEAF certification if you decide to go that way in the future.
- **Instructor Workshops** are fee based, and run by a **Pragmatic 365** Certified Consultant. As well as covering the content, there is also time for discussions about applying the content to your specific context.

PEAF 4 TOGAF

Why Should I Read This Book?

TOGAF® is a well known and "popular" Framework...

> "CERTIFICATION PASSES 100,000 MILESTONE"
>
> *- blog.opengroup.org/2020/06/23/togaf-9-certification-passes-100000-milestone*

But while there are many thousands of people certified in it, the number of people and Enterprises that actually use it, is much much lower. A lot of that has to do with the "badge appeal" in that it is something that people like to see on a CV, but a lot of it also has to do with the difficulty in adopting it. While TOGAF's strength lies in its detail, so does its weakness. PEAF strengths lies in its **Pragmatism**.

Who Should Read This Book?

Anyone who has taken TOGAF training and wants to use PEAF to Pragmatically adopt it, from CxO's and Directors to Database Support technicians. From Project Managers to Business Analysts. From Management Consultants to Programmers, and any one of a thousand other job titles that are (in whole or in part) concerned with the Transformation of Enterprises.

Why Should I attend a Workshop?

Run over 1 day and using this book, this Workshop introduces you to the parts of PEAF that can most pragmatically aid your adoption of TOGAF. Each part is mapped to the TOGAF sections and ADM allowing attendees to easily move between PEAF and TOGAF and vice versa.

If you have been on a TOGAF® workshop and are now wondering what to do, This workshop can help you.

This Workshop will provide you with the context and approach to give you that best chance of success.

Enterprise Transformation Assessment

Why Should I Read This Book?

Enterprises (Public Companies, Private Companies, Government Agencies) spend a lot of time and money on Transformation initiatives, however, most spend very little (if any) time and money on the MAGIC used. This lack of Transformation focus contributes to the widely accepted figures that 70% of all projects fail.

In the 21st Century, it is no longer enough just to be able to change. What matters now is how effective and efficient an Enterprise is at planning and executing that change. How an Enterprise effects Transformation has become a Strategic Strength where massive business opportunities can be gained, or a Strategic Weakness where massive business problems will result.

The **Pragmatic** Transformation Maturity Canvas (PTMC) Workshop is designed to enable Enterprises to effectively and efficiently perform a very **Pragmatic** maturity assessment of their Enterprise Transformation Capability.

Who Should Read This Book?

Anyone and everyone that is involved (in whole or in part) in the Transformation of Enterprises, from CxO's and Directors to Database Support technicians. From Project Managers to Business Analysts. From Management Consultants to Programmers, and any one of a thousand other job titles that are (in whole or in part) concerned with the Transformation of Enterprises.

Why Should I attend a Workshop?

Run over 1 day and using this book, the first part of the workshop presents the concepts required to understand the PTMC and why considering the maturity of your Enterprise Transformation capability is strategically important to its continued survival.

The remainder of the day is a hands-on workshop attendees use the PTMC to begin to consider and then expose the maturity of their Enterprise Transformation capability, and to develop overall findings and recommendations for its maturation.

Your Enterprises Transformation capability is strategically important to its survival.

This Workshop will provide you with an approach to assess it, and give you the best chance of maturing it in a Pragmatic way.

The Death of the Business and IT

Why Should I Read This Book?

Most Enterprises organise themselves around the tried and tested "Business" and "IT" way of thinking, and their departments and CxOs. This is understandable and has served us well over the years. However, this paradigm is no longer appropriate.

Who Should Read This Book?

Anyone and everyone that is involved (in whole or in part) in the Transformation of Enterprises, from CxO's and Directors to Database Support technicians. From Project Managers to Business Analysts. From Management Consultants to Programmers, and any one of a thousand other job titles that are (in whole or in part) concerned with the Transformation of Enterprises.

Why Should I attend a Workshop?

In the 21st century, the "IT" of an Enterprise is so inextricably linked to "The Business" of an Enterprise, it is impossible to decide where "The Business" stops and "IT" begins. In fact for many Enterprises today, "IT" is the business to a large extent. So, does this mean handing over the management and direction of the Enterprise to "IT"? No. that would be ludicrous, but so is thinking in terms of "The Business" and "IT". So what do we do? How can we square this circle? How can we think and organise enterprises in the 21st Century? The answer is to think in terms of Connecting the DOTS™

Run over 1 day and using this book, this workshop presents and defines DOTS. It discusses why thinking in terms of "The Business" and "IT" is no longer appropriate, and why adopting DOTS can ensure an Enterprise concentrates on, and be driven by, the core strategic capabilities of any Enterprise.

If you wish to make sure your Enterprise can excel in the 21st century, it is imperative that it focusses on its key strategic capabilities.

This workshop will provide you with the context and approach to give you that best chance of success.

Enterprise Transformation Governance

Why Should I Read This Book?

Many Enterprises already have some kind of governance with respect to Enterprise Transformation. Sadly, many of the Methods (and Artefacts) employed are deeply flawed. Governance tends to be either a tick in the box exercise or a policing exercise. Having witnessed the failure of many Transformation/change initiatives over 35 years, I have created a new way of effecting Governance, with addition of the crucial Lobbying component that is missing in most Enterprises. The changes required to utilise Enterprise Debt™ are small but the effects can be truly game changing. If the Management decides to control (manage) Transformation Debt™, then this book sets out all that is required to do so. Pragmatically.

Enterprises (Public Companies, Private Companies, Government Agencies) spend Billions of Dollars year on year Transforming and changing themselves. With widely accepted figures of 70% of all projects fail (McKinsey, September 2013) the amount of money (and more importantly time) that is lost cannot continue, especially in a world that is changing faster and faster while demanding that all this Transformation must be done with less resource.

Identifying and managing Transformation Debt™ (that is created when Transformation work deviates from accepted Roadmaps and Principles) is the key to keeping your Transformation projects aligned with your Strategy and identifying when any deviations occur at the point when that deviation occurs so that sound business decisions can me made to either accept the deviation with a plan of how to deal with the resulting issues and risks, or to act to stop the deviation.

Who Should Read This Book?

Anyone who wants to stop wasting time and money and reduce the number of project failures. E.g. CIOs, Head of PMO, Head of Business Analysis, Head of S&A, Head of Solution Delivery, Enterprise Architects, Solution Architects, Business Analysts, Project Managers, Developers, Testers, Configuration Managers, Change Managers, etc, etc.

Why Should I attend a Workshop?

Pragmatic Approach to Enterprise Transformation Governance.

Run over 1 day and using this book, the first part of the workshop presents the concepts required to understand Transformation Debt™ and provides a detailed method for defining, measuring and managing it.

The remainder of the day is a hands-on workshop where you will think about the principles that are applicable to your Enterprise, practise defining the Transformation Debt™ when those principles are violated, and making decisions to accept the debt created or provide the resources required.

Transformation Debt™ is a fact.

Your Transformation efforts are creating it every day.

Either you will control it.

Or it will control you.

Enterprise Transformation Culture

Why Should I Read This Book?

Enterprises (Public Companies, Private Companies, Government Agencies) spend a lot of money on Transformation initiatives, and in trying to mature how they plan and execute those initiatives. A lot of time and money is spent on processes and IT tools to help an Enterprise plan and run projects better. However, after all this time and money is spent, processes are changed, new tools are bought and installed, still the overall numbers are that 70% of all projects fail. How can this be? The simple answer is that the culture at large in most Enterprise Transformation capabilities (the unwritten rules and regulations) are perfectly engineered to produce a 70% failure rate. So put away your tools, and start thinking about culture today.

Culture trumps Everything™ is much much more than just a saying. It is a very cold hard fact, which if ignored, literally has the capacity to destroy civilisations.

Who Should Read This Book?

Anyone and everyone that is involved (in whole or in part) in the Transformation of Enterprises, from CxO's and Directors to Database Support technicians. From Project Managers to Business Analysts. From Management Consultants to Programmers, and any one of a thousand other job titles that are (in whole or in part) concerned with the Transformation of Enterprises.

Why Should I attend a Workshop?

Run over 1 day and using this book, the workshop exposes the culture that exists in many enterprises. It gets the attendees thinking in terms of culture, different ways to think about it, the role psychology plays, how the two tribes of "the business" and "IT" contrast, and over 40 keypoints to help focus the mind.

Your Enterprise is already spending a lot of money on Transformation initiatives, and so it is imperative that your Enterprise stands the best chance of reducing the 70% failure rate.

This Workshop will provide you with the context and approach to give you that best chance of success.

Enterprise Architecture Tools

Why Should I Read This Book?

Many Enterprises already have some kind of EA Modelling Tool, that are being actively used for the purpose of Enterprise Architecture, aka creating and maintaining Structural (Capability) and Transformational (Portfolio) Roadmaps. But those Enterprises are in the minority.

Many, many more have either no EA Modelling Tool at all, or they have one but have found that it has not lived up to expectations and sits gathering dust on the shelf or being used as glorified reporting tool and generally providing questionable (if any) returns.

Having witnessed many failures, this book sets out the Methods, Artefacts and Environment required to effectively choose and operate an EA Modelling Tool. It covers the key things that must be done to effectively and efficiently choose a tool, and then to operate it in a sustainable way.

If the Management decides to choose (or replace) and operate an EA modelling tool effectively, then this book sets out all that is required to do so. Pragmatically.

Who Should Read This Book?

Anyone involved in making sure their investment in an EA Modelling Tool is sound. E.g. CIOs, Head of PMO, Head of Business Analysis, Head of S&A, Head of Solution Delivery, Enterprise Architects, Solution Architects, Business Analysts, Project Managers, Configuration Managers, Change Managers, etc, etc.

Why Should I attend a Workshop?

Run over 1 day and using this book, the first part of the workshop presents the concepts required to understand an EA Modelling Tool, what it used for, what information must be modelled, and **Pragmatic** methods for adoption and use.

The remainder of the day is a hands-on workshop where you will formulate your own tailored approach for selection, define which requirements are key to you, and develop a shortlist.

Enterprises (Public Companies, Private Companies, Government Agencies) spend a lot of time and money on tools. But many of these tools sit on the shelf or are used in only small ways.

The most common reasons are that:

The tool they selected is not is not appropriate for their Enterprise.

The way the tool is being used is not appropriate for their Enterprise.

If you are going to be spending a lot of money on a tool, it is imperative that the project stands the best chance of success.

This Workshop will provide you with the context and approach to give you that best chance of success.

What is Enterprise Architecture

Why Should I Read This Book?

Enterprises (Public Companies, Private Companies, Government Agencies) spend a lot of money on Enterprise Architecture. But the world is so full of myths, half-truths and misinterpretations, they rarely get to understand what it actually is, much less how to use it. EA has the capacity to massively increase the effectiveness, efficiency, agility and sustainability of an Enterprises transformation portfolio.

Enterprise Architecture has existed (in many forms) for a long time, and there are many "experts" around to educate others. However, EA is currently at the same point in time, as Chemistry was when Chemists were Alchemists. So perhaps a better term for Enterprise Architecture is Enterprise Alchemy and a better term for Enterprise Architects is Enterprise Alchemists. (It is perhaps serendipitous that the acronym is the same!)) The parallels between what EA claims and what alchemy claimed are intriguing.

That may see flippant or a pathetic attempt at humour, however, in admitting that, as a profession, EA is about as mature as alchemy was hundreds of years ago, we have made the most important step of all. The first step. We have stopped being unconsciously incompetent and we are now concisely incompetent. Admitting that EA is as mature as Alchemy is big thing. Many people will not agree (mostly the Alchemists!). Many people have a vested interest in presenting themselves and their companies as "experts" even when their expertise just turns out to be "whatever we think".

The time has come for a change. The time has come for Enterprise Alchemy to grow up and Become Enterprise Architecture. This book presents information to define Enterprise Architecture, and Architects in a Pragmatic fashion. It does not purport to be the end of the road. But it does try to be the beginning.

Who Should Read This Book?

Anyone and everyone that is involved (in whole or in part) in the Transformation of Enterprises, from CxO's and Directors to Database Support technicians. From Project Managers to Business Analysts. From Management Consultants to Programmers, and any one of a thousand other job titles that are (in whole or in part) concerned with the Transformation of Enterprises.

Why Should I attend a Workshop?

Run over 1 day and using this book, the workshop presents what EA is (the noun and the verb), what EA is not (the noun and the verb), how EA fits into the wider Transformation domain, how the popular frameworks such as Zachman, TOGAF, POET, PEAF, COBIT and ITIL fit in, the fundamental differences between Architecture & Engineering, the two types of Enterprise Architect (the role) and over 50 keypoints to help focus the mind.

KEYPOINT:

PEAF Focused Workshops, allow you to focus on specific areas.

ADOPTION:

Management: Engage Pragmatic EC to deliver Focussed training.

Questions to Ponder

- Have you read any of these books?
- If so, what did you like? What did you not like?
- Have you been on any of these workshops?
- If so, what did you like? What did you not like?
- Which course would interest you the most?

Introduction > Training > Options

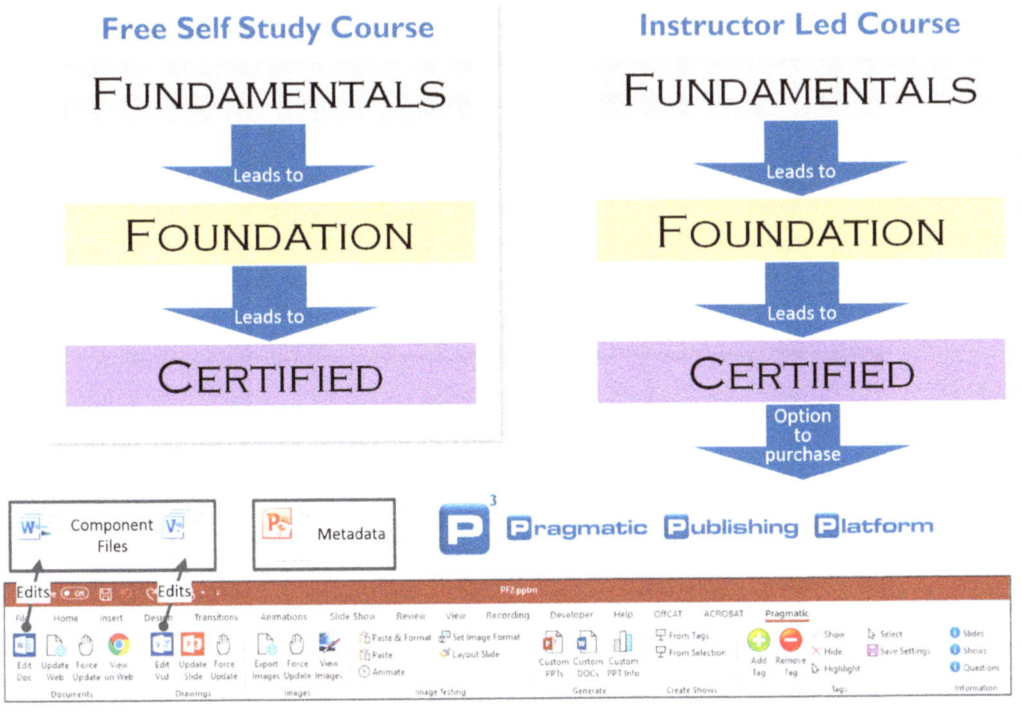

The progression from Fundamentals through Foundation to Certified is the same for people opting for Self Study or Instructor Led training.

In addition, Enterprises that have completed the Instructor Led course are also able to buy (as an option) the **Pragmatic P**ublishing **P**latform (**P3**), to allow them to create and modify Frameworks in an efficient and seamless way.

KEYPOINT:

Access to the Pragmatic Publishing Platform is granted by graduating from an Instructor led course.

ADOPTION:

EA Project Team: Attend Instructor led training, to gain access to the Publishing Platform and all component files.files.

Questions to Ponder

- Which type of course would you choose?
- Do you think a better understanding could be gained from an Instructor led course?
- What are the benefits of each type of course?

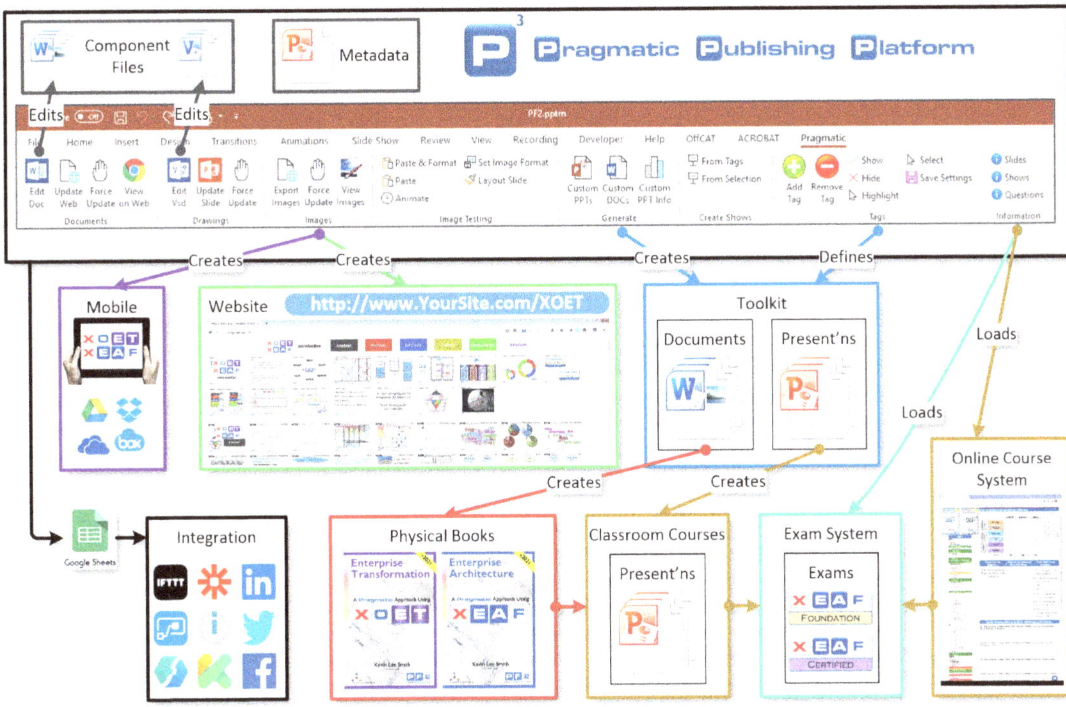

The **Pragmatic Publishing Platform** (**P3**) is available for purchase separately and exists in two versions:

- A **Standalone Version** – with no content, allowing people to create and maintain any content they wish, that results in the creation of training presentations, associated exams, websites and books.
- A **Pragmatic Version** – which include 100% of the base material in all of **Pragmatic** frameworks – currently PF2, POET and PEAF, allowing people to rebrand and modify as they wish.

P3 comprises a coherent environment which automates much of the administrative tasks related to the production and maintenance of the base material and the creation of custom material. The platform uses MS PowerPoint as its base, utilising a custom **Pragmatic** Ribbon to allow users to manage the material.

- **Documents** – Allow the maintenance of the words for each component.
- **Drawings – Allow the maintenance of the drawings for each component.**
- **Images – Allows the generation of images.** Separate .png files are exported in five different resolutions - one for Books, three for the website (thumbnail, normal and hi-res) and one for the export folder.
- **Image Testing – Allows supplementary functions for testing image generation.**
- **Generate - Allow the generation of PowerPoint and Word Toolkit documents**
- **Create Shows – Allows the creation of shows using tags or the selection**

- **Tags – Allows the manipulation and visualisation of tags which define each show.**
- **Component Files**- These files constitute the master files of the Framework or Ontology that all other files are created from. Each component is composed of a Visio file for the graphic and a Word document for the words.
- **Metadata** – This information (per component) is held in tags within the Notes of each slide. It comprises Show indicators, Keypoints, Questions, Answers, Adoption Statements and Reader Questions.
- **Toolkit** – From these Components, any number of Documents and PowerPoint Presentations can be easily created, based on a selection of the Components.
- **Website** - Easily integrate your framework (images and words) with your intranet to promote understanding and adoption.
- **Mobile** - The images of your framework are automatically exported to a folder (e.g. Dropbox) that can be synchronised to mobile devices, allowing you to carry the core of your framework with you at all times, to promote understanding and adoption.
- **Books** – From the Book documents, physical books can be easily created.
- **Training Courses** – Training courses consisting of presentations to be used in classroom training and information loaded into an online course system. In addition an online examination system is loaded with exam questions.
- **Integration** – Component Information is synchronised to Google Sheets, which can then in turn, integrate though any integration application to, for example, Facebook, Twitter, LinkedIn etc for publishing of changes or daily messages.

KEYPOINT:

P3 allows Enterprises to easily produce and maintain their own Frameworks and publish them to books, their intranet and mobile devices.

ADOPTION:

Management: Adopt the Pragmatic Publishing Platform to streamline your Pragmatic X-Framework adoption.

Questions to Ponder

- What do you currently use to maintain and publish the frameworks your Enterprise uses?
- What other uses can you think of for the Pragmatic Publishing Platform?

Introduction > Pragmatic Publishing Platform > Design

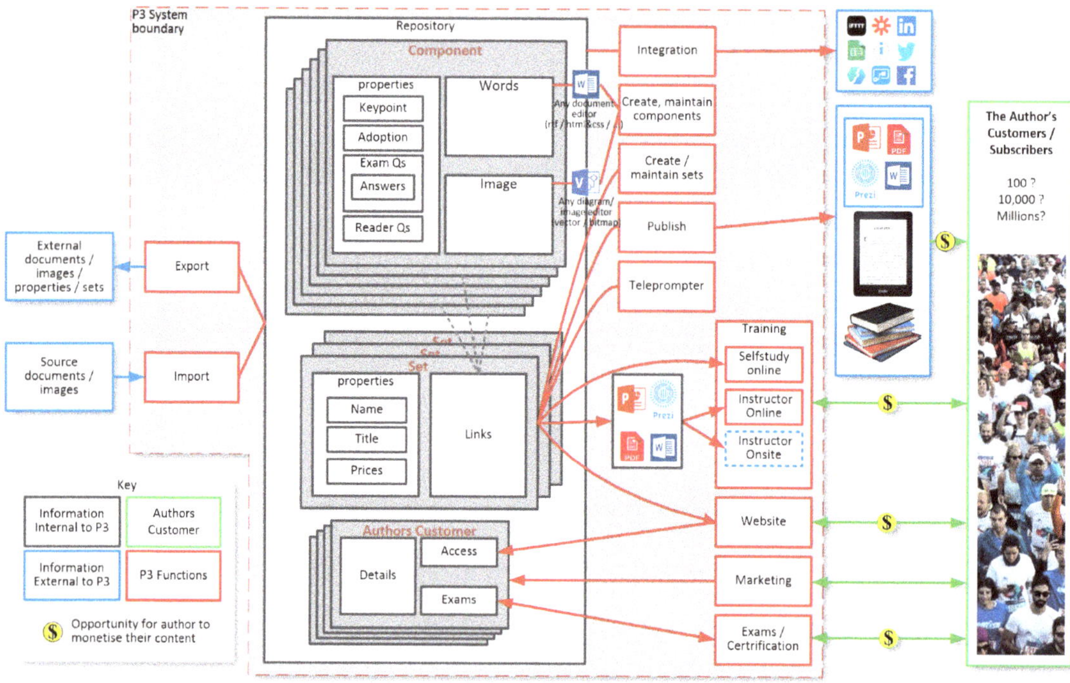

P3 is a component-based knowledge authoring and publishing system. All content is constructed from components. A component is whatever the author wants a component to be, however it is suggested that each component teach people one important concept or thing. More complicated things should be broken down into other components. Each component consists of three distinct pieces of information:

- **Words** – Authored in any document editor such as Microsoft Word, and in any format such as rtf or html.
- **Images** – Authored in any image editor such as Visio, and in any format such as raster (e.g. png, gif, jpg) or vector (e.g. vsd, wmf)
- **Properties**
  - Name (as part of a navigation structure)
  - Keypoint – The key thought or point that the reader should take away from this component.
  - Adoption – A list of things to do in order to adopt the component.
  - Exam Questions – One or more exam questions to test the knowledge of someone learning the component.
  - Exam Answers – For each question, 1 correct answer and any number of wrong answers, to allow a multiple choice examination to be conducted. (The exam subsystem allows for both multiple choice exams and written exams)

In addition, the repository contains two other important parts.

Firstly Sets. Sets collect components together for the purposes of publishing and training.

- Links – a list of links to components included in the set and the order that is required.
- Properties
  - Name – The Authors internal quick name of the set
  - Title – The title to be used when published
  - Prices – The prices of things published for example print books, Kindle books, training courses.

Secondly, Authors Customer.

- Details - Information about the authors customers/subscribers, such as name, email address etc.
- Access – Information about what content the authors customer has accessed and when.
- Exams – Information about what courses and exams the user has subscribed to.

All of this information is owned and controlled by the Author and can be exported at any time, in a variety of formats (words documents, image files, sets, etc) such that the Author always owns their content.

In addition, to aid adoption of the platform, Authors can import their existing knowledge in a variety of formats with automatic splitting of large documents into components by using some identifying data such as headings or page breaks.

- Functionality
- Integration
- Create, Maintain, Components
- Create, Maintain Sets
- Publish
- Training
- Website
- Marketing
- Exams / Certification

Customer Segments

- Worldwide - Platform akin to YouTube for thinkers.
    - Best practice
    - Stories for children/learning
- Companies – To document the MAGIC of their business, for onboarding or general change management teaching/rollout.
- Universities - For professors to author content for students.

Why would an author want to use P3?

People who tick 1 or more of these boxes:

- Have a reasonably large set of information/knowledge
- Need flexibility to easily evolve/maintain it over time
- Want to share/publish their content on the internet/intranet
- Want to publish their content to eBook or Print
- Want to be able to easily slice and dice their content into focus areas.
- Want to offer training (offline, online, onsite) to people.
- Want to offer exams/certification to people.
- Want to automatically push their content out via twitter, likedin, facebook etc
- Want to build a following of subscribers who like their content

P3 can be used to create, maintain, and publish any type of information for any domain of interest:

- Best Practice
    - Management
    - Enterprise Architecture
    - Drilling oil wells
    - Banking
    - Pharma…
- Sales play books
- Stories

The content can be structured around any domains you like, although P3 provides 5 fundamental MAGIC domains for grouping best practice information:

- Methods - Methodologies
- Artefacts - Ontologies
- Guidance – Principles, policies, Standards…
- Items - Technologies
- Culture - Ethics, Values, Roles…

It provides a consistent updated taxonomy of knowledge that can be shared across all out-puts and to all of the people (customers) using the content that it creates and manages.

Competitors

Before P3 was written, I spent some time looking for a component based publishing platform. At that time I discovered AuthorIT https://www.author-it.com/ but after spending some time to review it by actively use it, it became obvious that it could not meet my needs.

> **KEYPOINT:**
>
> P3 is a component based authoring system.

> **ADOPTION:**
>
> Management: Adopt the Pragmatic Publishing Platform to streamline your Pragmatic X-Framework adoption.

Questions to Ponder

- What do you currently use to maintain and publish the frameworks your Enterprise uses?
- What other uses can you think of for the Pragmatic Publishing Platform?

Language

KEYPOINT:

The Language section of PEFF introduces fundamental terminology that is used throughout Pragmatic's Frameworks.

Questions to Ponder

- Do you think fundamental language is useful to your Enterprise?
- What fundamental language does your Enterprise use?
- If none, what fundamental language do you think would be appropriate?

FACT 1

I guarantee that SOME or ALL of the words used here will NOT be consistent with your current definitions.

FACT 2

I guarantee that ALL of the words used here ARE consistent within this framework.

The **Pragmatic** Family of Frameworks are written in English and you would therefore expect to be able to understand every word.

However, although most of us speak English fluently, the same cannot be said about the language we use to talk, about things in relation to Enterprises.

Different people use different words to mean different things at different times. This is a massive problem, which makes understanding anything anyone says, at best impossible, and at worst, apparently possible. (It's worse when apparently possible, because that's when people think they understand each other, but don't)

People, including me, get attached to the meaning of the words we use, and defend those meanings passionately. This is totally understandable, because the meanings we attach to words, are the absolute basis for our understanding things.

Pragmatic has no desire or wish to impose our meaning of words onto you, however, for the purposes of understanding the **Pragmatic** Family of Frameworks, I would ask you to temporarily put aside your current meanings of words, and try to embrace, accept and understand the meanings of the words used here. The actual words are not so important as the meaning behind them.

Many words people use are overloaded with multiple meanings, and when this is not clear (i.e. a lot of the time!) communication can become quite confusing, not to say heated.

Sometimes we need to use different language to explain a difficult concept. For example, let's look at an explanation of the offside rule in football (or soccer to those of you from across the pond – see, there's that language problem again!) to someone who knows nothing about the rules of football, but knows everything about the rules of buying shoes…

"You're in a shoe shop, second in the queue for the till. Behind the shop assistant on the till is a pair of shoes which you have seen and which you must have.
The shopper in front of you has seen them also and is eyeing them with desire. But, both of you have forgotten your wallets.
It would (of course) be rude to push in front of the shopper in front of you, if you had no money to pay for the shoes.
(The shop assistant remains at the till waiting.)
Your friend is trying on another pair of shoes at the back of the shop and sees your dilemma.
They prepare to throw their wallet to you.
If they do, you can catch the wallet, then walk round the other shopper and buy the shoes!
At a pinch your friend could throw the wallet ahead of the other shopper, and "whilst it is in flight" you could nip around the other shopper, catch the wallet, and buy the shoes!
BUT, you must always remember that until the wallet has "actually been thrown", it would be just plain wrong for you to move in front of the other shopper and buy the shoes.

- Anonymous

So, if English can be confusing to people who speak it natively, imagine the problems in the multinational world we live in, as we can see in this explanation of Cricket (in a world without boundaries - pun intended), ...

"You have two sides, one out in the field and one in.
Each person that's in the side that's in goes out, and when he's out he comes in and the next person goes in until he's out.
When they are all out, the side that's out comes in and the side that's been in goes out and tries to get those coming in, out. Sometimes you get people still in and not out.
When a person goes out to go in, the people who are out try to get him out, and when he is out he goes in and the next person in goes out and goes in.
There are two people called umpires who stay out all the time and they decide when the people who are in are out.
When both sides have been in and all the people have been out, and both sides have been out twice after all the people have been in, including those who are not out, that is the end of the game."

- Anonymous

KEYPOINT:

Be ever vigilant of the hidden confusion that language can create.

ADOPTION:

EA Project Team: Create a data dictionary for all the terms used in the Enterprise's Transformation Capability.

Questions to Ponder

- Do people in your enterprise speak the same language?
- Are you prepared to map the content of The Pragmatic Family of Frameworks to your own internal naming conventions?
- If not what changes would you make to The Pragmatic Family of Frameworks?

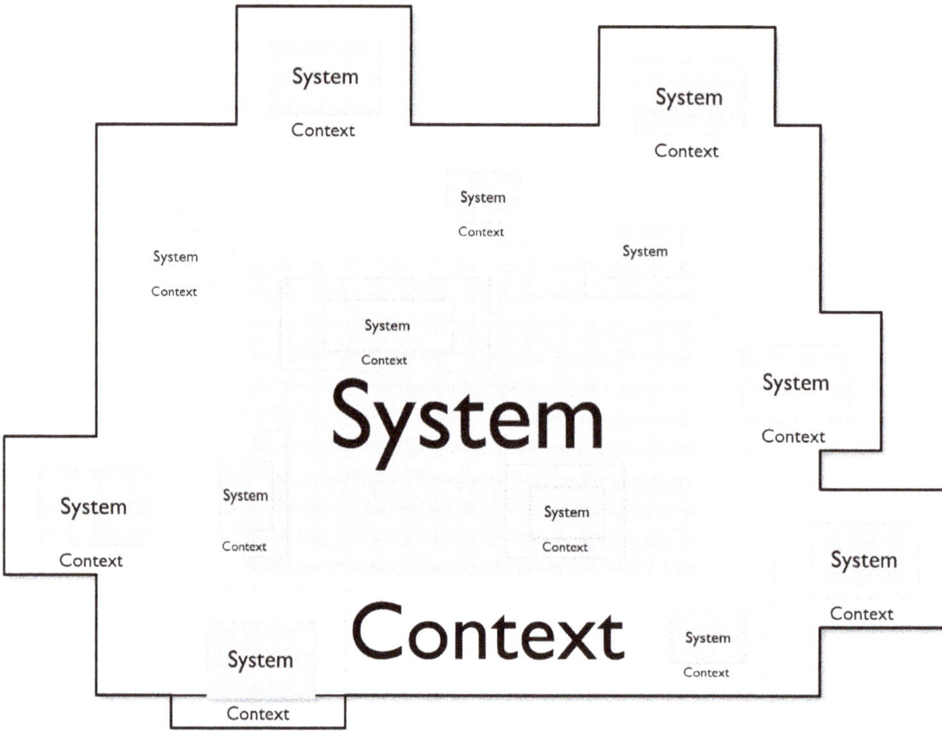

When we use the word "System" we use it to refer to anything. Literally any "Thing".

- It can refer to physical things, like a car, a boat, a molecule, a planet, etc.
- It can refer to non-physical things, like processes, thoughts or computer programs.
- It can also refer to things which are a mixture of the two, like an Enterprise, or part of an Enterprise.

Whatever the System is, that System always exists within a Context.

The Context is not a thing in itself, but instead is formed by other Systems (in part or in whole) that are not considered to be part of that System, but have some connection or relationship to it. For example they influence it, or are influenced by it.

This basic concept of a System existing within a context, is also defined in an International Standard, ISO42010. Although its title is "Systems and Software Engineering", and there are numerous and constant references to, and examples of IT Systems, 95% of it applies equally to the Architecture of Systems in any domain. It's unfortunate that it is so IT focussed, because it perpetuates the common myth that Enterprise Architecture is **only** about IT, and the things connected to IT.

The overwhelming desire of any system is one of self-preservation, which includes preservation of its structure - which is why many systems (and the people that operate within them) resist change.

A key thing to understand about any system is that it WILL be abused, especially any system that people participate in, be it at work, the tax system, the healthcare system, the social care system, etc.

People who are accountable for a system (e.g. management) tend to make two invalid and deeply damaging assumptions:

1) Firstly, they assume that the system they have put in place will not be abused. That is not to say that they have not thought about how the system will be abused, and put in place things to stop that abuse, of course they have. The problems come from not accepting that even with all the measures they have put in place, the system will still be abused.
2) Secondly, they think that when new types of abuse are exposed, that the solution to that problem is to put in place more and more detailed checks and balances. What is not realised, is that they are increasing complexity, and as complexity increases, so does the opportunity for abuse. A better approach, would be to look more at the fundamentals and aim to reduce complexity, thereby reducing the opportunity for abuse.

So, if we accept that the number of opportunities to abuse a system that **Actually Exists** is always larger than the number of opportunities that we **Think Exists** and have catered for, there will always be a number of **Opportunities for Abuse**. The only argument is what is the relationship between the number that we **Think Exists** vs the number that **Actually Exists**. The function is definitely not linear and more likely polynomial in nature. So, if you want to reduce the opportunities to abuse a system, you need to reduce the complexity of that system.

This is illustrated in the table below. As we can see, things break down pretty rapidly. You could argue that a polynomial function is not the correct function to apply, but one thing you have to admit is, the opportunity to abuse a system is always greater than opportunities we think exist.

Think Exists	Actually Exists	Opportunities for Abuse
4	6	2
6	15	9
15	105	90
105	5460	5355
5460	14903070	14897610
14903070	1.11051E+14	1.11051E+14

KEYPOINT:

Everything is a System.

ADOPTION:

EA Project Team: Add the definition of "System" to the data dictionary used in the Enterprise's Transformation Capability.

Questions to Ponder

- What Systems does your Enterprise use and operate that are not IT Systems?
- Has anyone outside of IT heard of or read ISO42010?
- If not, who will you introduce ISO42010 to tomorrow?
- When correcting problems, does your Enterprise add complexity or reduce it?
- What function would you use to relate the number of opportunities for abusing a system to the number of opportunities we think exists and have catered for?
- You are a System. What makes up your context?

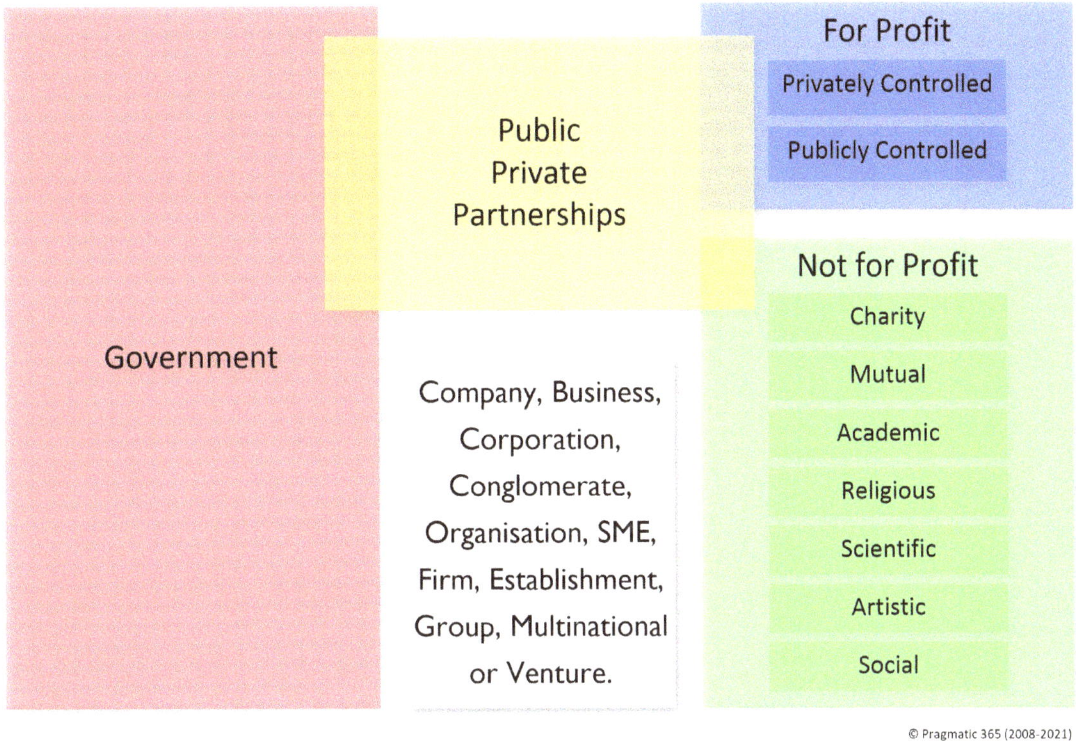

An Enterprise is a type of System.

The word Enterprise is used as a general noun - to refer to things such as public and private companies, government agencies, charities, universities etc. This is not an exhaustive list but illustrates the point. In addition we use the word Enterprise as a general noun in place of many other words people may use to refer to each these "types". For example, a Private Company may be called a Company, Business, Corporation, Conglomerate, Organisation, SME, Firm, Establishment, Group, Multinational or Venture. We use the word Enterprise to refer to them all.

An Enterprise is a system and therefore every Enterprise also has an Enterprise Context.

Many people take a different view (citing TOGAF) which is that an Enterprise could be anything, e.g. a department, a smaller part of a company, etc, and from a purists point of view they are correct but only if you use the word Enterprise as synonym for the word System, rather than to describe a specific type of system - an Enterprise. To support that view they refer to TOGAF's Preliminary Stage which states as one of its objectives is "To identify and scope the elements of the enterprise organizations affected by the business directive and define the constraints and assumptions (particularly in a federated architecture environment)" i.e. to restrict the scope of EA to something that could well be a smaller part of the entire Enterprise and to further restrict that to "the business directive".

This is borne out by the rest of TOGAF which is Project Architecture based rather than Enterprise Architecture based. However, TOGAF (on page 25 - section 3.34) defines and Enterprise as "The highest level (typically) of description of an organization and typically covers all missions and functions. An enterprise will often span multiple organizations." which appears to tie in with our definition above. This is one of the many conflicts and inconsistencies within TOGAF. It says it is an Enterprise Architecture framework, goes on to define an Enterprise as being typically an organisation (as described by **Pragmatic**) but then goes on to state that the first act is to de-scope the entire Enterprise to something smaller - and restrict work to a "business directive" at which point it is no longer Enterprise Architecture but a sub part of the Enterprise and moves forward from that single transformation project perspective which makes it project level and not Enterprise Level.

KEYPOINT:

The Word Enterprise does not mean "large" or "large IT" or "senior". It is a general noun.

ADOPTION:

EA Project Team: Add the definition of "Enterprise" to the data dictionary used in the Enterprise's Transformation Capability.

Questions to Ponder

- Does your Enterprise use the word Enterprise to refer to many types of things?
- If not, what other words are used and what are their definitions?
- Is there a common understanding?
- If not, what problems does that create?

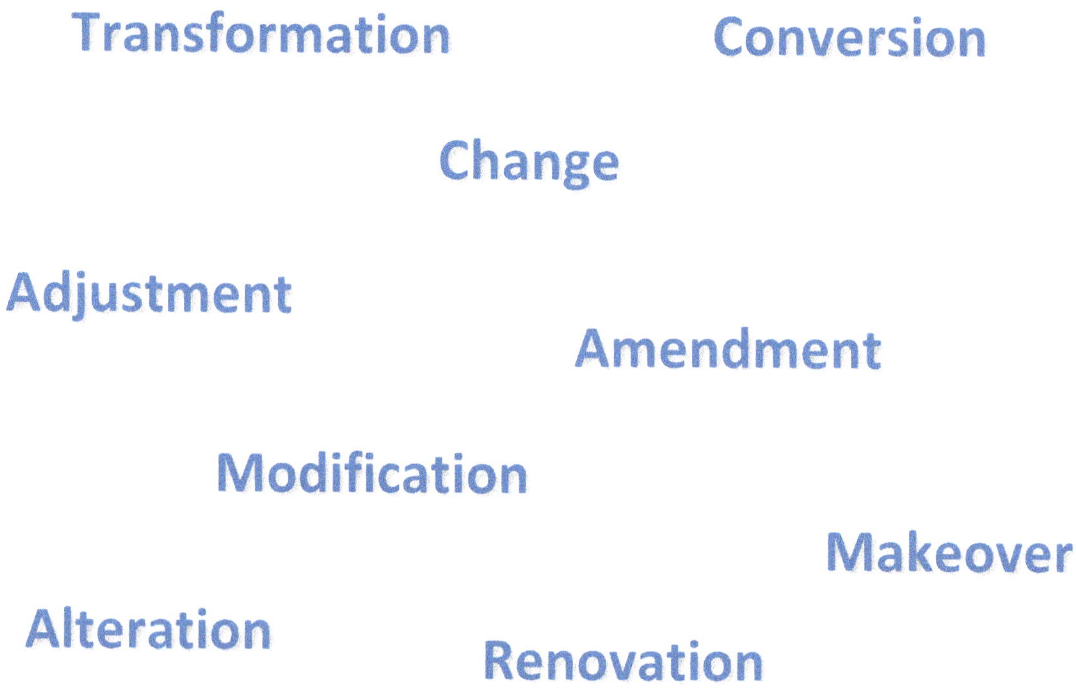

It can be easily misinterpreted (and often is) how **Pragmatic** uses the word Transformation.

It is possible for people to believe that the word Transformation (as we use it) is used specifically because it means something different to the word change. Here's a quote from Patrick on LinkedIn illustrating how many people confuse **Pragmatic**'s use of the word Transformation:

> "I don't believe that Organisations are under a constant pressure to transform, but they are under pressure to change. I think there is a fundamental difference between change and transformation. Transformation is the re-inventing of an Organisation and effects the majority of the organisation itself. Change is more subjective and specific in nature and delivery. Therefore transformation is NOT a normal event within an organisation and therefore doesn't require a permanent "C" position"
>
> ***- Patrick (LinkedIn)***

Pragmatic makes no such distinction. We use the word Transformation to mean any and all change. A general noun to refer to many other nouns that, at a fundamental level, mean the same thing.

KEYPOINT:

There is no hidden connotation to Pragmatic's use of the word "Transformation".

ADOPTION:

EA Project Team: Add the definition of "Transformation" to the data dictionary used in the Enterprise's Transformation Capability.

Questions to Ponder

- Does your Enterprise use the word Transformation to refer to a specific type of change?
- If not, what other words are used and what are their definitions?
- Is there a common understanding?
- If not, what problems does that create?

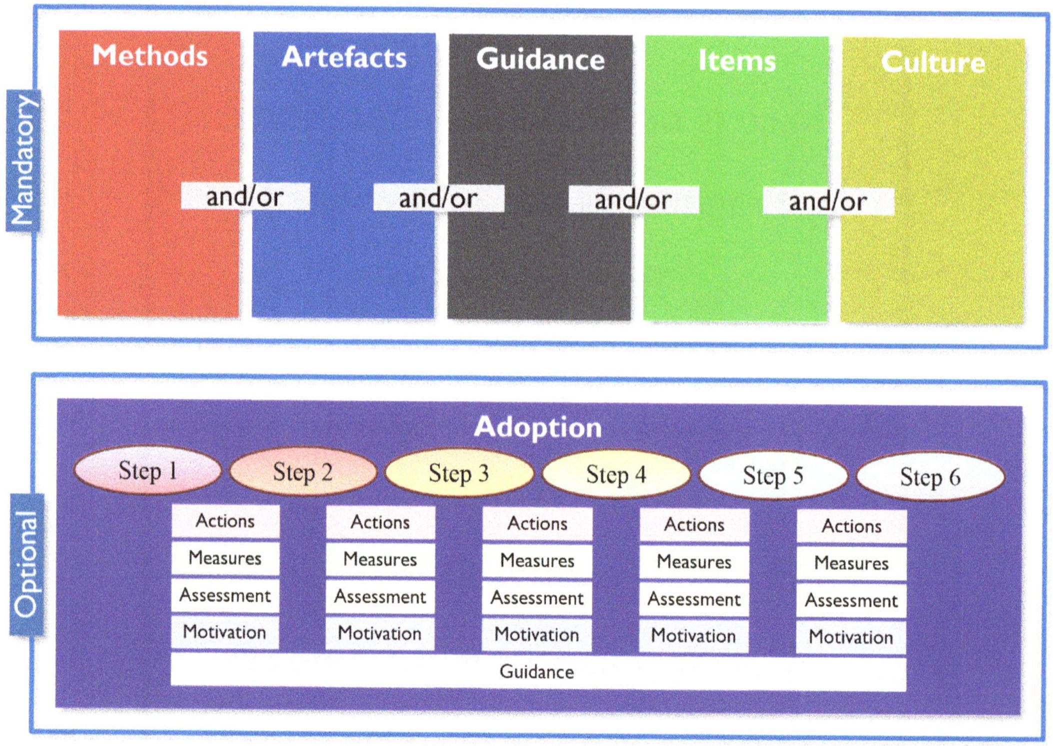

What is a Framework?

This is a common question and one that has almost as many answers (if not more!) as the eternal "What is EA?" question.

All Frameworks exist to improve the way something is done (i.e. to increase the effectiveness and efficiency and to reduce the risk of failure). In many respects they are an expression of "Best Practice". They contain different types of things depending upon the purpose of the framework - its domain.

More specifically, Frameworks are composed of information relating to:

- **Methods** (e.g. processes, practices, etc) and/or
- **Artefacts** (e.g. Ontologies, Metamodels, Reference Models, Product Descriptions etc) and/or
- **Guidance** (e.g. Principles, Policies, Standards, etc) and/or
- **Items** (e.g. Tools, Frameworks, etc) and/or
- **Culture** (e.g. People, Culture, Values, Psychology, etc)

There must be at least one thing in at least one of these areas for it to be a framework.

A Framework may optionally also contain:

- **Adoption** (e.g. Actions regarding which Steps to take to adopt it, and for each step, what the Measures, Assessment and Motivation for moving to the next step are.)

Some frameworks only contain one of the above (e.g. Zachman is only an Ontology - an Artefact).

Some frameworks contain some of the above (e.g. TOGAF has No information on Culture or Adoption.

And some frameworks contain all of the above (e.g. POET and PEAF).

Many people take the view that a framework consists only of Artefact information, e.g. meta-models, ontologies, reference models, etc. This tends to be a very engineering, IT and data, myopic view. This view is plainly not true. Frameworks can contain all of the things that MAGIC and MAGMA define. For example, There are legal Frameworks, political Frameworks, cultural Frameworks, analysis Frameworks, architectural Frameworks, management Frameworks, business Frameworks, project management Frameworks, software development Frameworks, governance Frameworks, modelling Frameworks, etc, etc, etc. They may or may not have some information relating to meta-models or meta-meta-models or ontologies etc, but they are all frameworks - even the ones with no meta-model.

KEYPOINT:

A Framework is an expression of Best Practice comprising information in at least one area (Methods, Artefacts, Guidance, Items, Culture) and optionally information regarding its Adoption.

ADOPTION:

Enterprise Architect: Categorise the content of any Framework you use, in terms of Context + MAGIC + Adoption.

Questions to Ponder

- How do you define a framework?
- What kinds of things would you put in a Framework?
- What Frameworks do you know and what types of things do they contain?

"In theory, there is no difference between theory and practice. But, in practice, there is."

- Jan L. A. van de Snepscheut / Yogi Berra

Pragmatic's Ontologies and Frameworks can easily be thought of some ivory tower academic tomes which are nice in a perfect world but does not provide any practical advice.

People ask me...

> "Yeah! It's great but, does it tell me and others exactly what to do, when, how and with what?"

Usually closely followed by...

> "It's not detailed enough to be useful."

The answer is no. That is exactly what they were designed not to do.

Yes, there is a difference between theory and practice. In practice detail will be exposed and problems will be found that means we cannot follow the theory literally and to the letter, but theory is never meant to be applied literally and so why people complain when it's not I am not sure. It's almost like people want theory to be practice, which if it was, it wouldn't be theory anymore!

In the world, there is no lack of things telling people exactly what to do with excruciating detail (look at some other frameworks out there) and while detail is good, detail that is not framed in theory is either foolhardy or just plain dangerous. Balance is the key. We call that a **Pragmatic** approach.

Theory is more about thinking than doing and practice is more about doing than thinking. The intimation that if something is "theory" it is useless and not worth looking at is ludicrous, but people do it all the time and use it as way to dismiss things. Maybe it's a sign of the times we live in where doing things is the only thing people seem to care about - thinking doesn't seem to have any value anymore. Which is really strange since thinking is exactly what humans are best at.

The truth is, everything you see around you was built on theory.

Theory provides a context for **practice** to happen within.

By exposing the fundamentals of transformation and defining patterns that link all the parts into a holistic whole we give people the context to work within that continuum cooperatively. It's like driving a car, you don't teach someone to drive a car by telling them how to turn the steering wheel (left a bit, right a bit, a bit more, too much, go a bit left, a bit more….) you explain and show what the steering wheel and other controls do and how they interrelate, understanding the physics involved and getting them to feel the physics involved (e.g. what happens if you turn the steering wheel fast at high speed as compared to slow speed) and that provides the context.

KEYPOINT:

Theory is just as important as Practice

ADOPTION:

Management: Don't dismiss theory as not important.

Questions to Ponder

- Is someone telling you when to turn the steering wheel and how much?
- Does your Enterprise provide you with things that allow you to understand how you fit into the overall Transformation domain?
- If not, would your job be more effective, efficient and more rewarding if it did?
- Who will you lobby to provide it?

Language > Basics > Colours

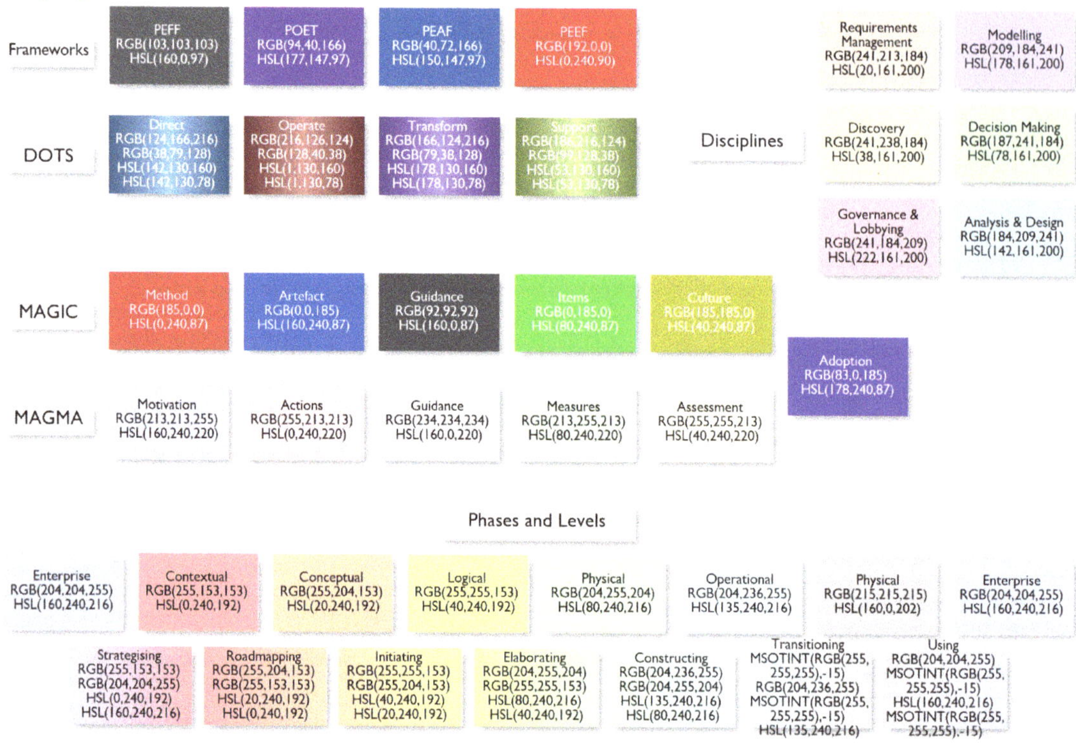

Here we detail Pragmatic's use of colour. Colour is not used to make think look pretty.

Pragmatic uses colour to aid peoples understanding as colour is an excellent way for the mind to quickly take in and relate information.

Some people like to see colour (information) others see it as extraneous and creating more confusion that clarity. Others like colour but just not like Pragmatic's choice of colour and would change them in certain ways, such as making them more muted, or only using colour to represent the type of thing – e.g. instead of using the 40 colours shown here, use one colour for each set of colours.

Whatever your preference, using P3 (Pragmatic Publishing Platform) allows you to easily change the colours to anything you prefer. In addition, users of the website can elect to see the diagrams in full colour, or one of a set of themed colours such as shades of blue or orange or grey.

KEYPOINT:

Colour

=

Information

=

Understanding.

ADOPTION:

EA Project Team: Use standardised colours to mean something.

Questions to Ponder

- Do you like Pragmatic's use of colour?
- If not, what would you change?

Culture

KEYPOINT:

The Culture section of POET defines the roles and the culture required.

ADOPTION:

C-Suite: Instigate a review of the Culture at play in the Enterprise's Transformation Capability, to determine if it's maturity is appropriate.

Questions to Ponder

- With respect to your Enterprises Transformation capability, what Culture exists?
- Is the Culture documented? Understood?
- Is it fit for purpose?
- Are they used? All the time? Only when it suits?
- What parts are Good? Why? Bad? Why?

Culture > Organisation Structure > Management

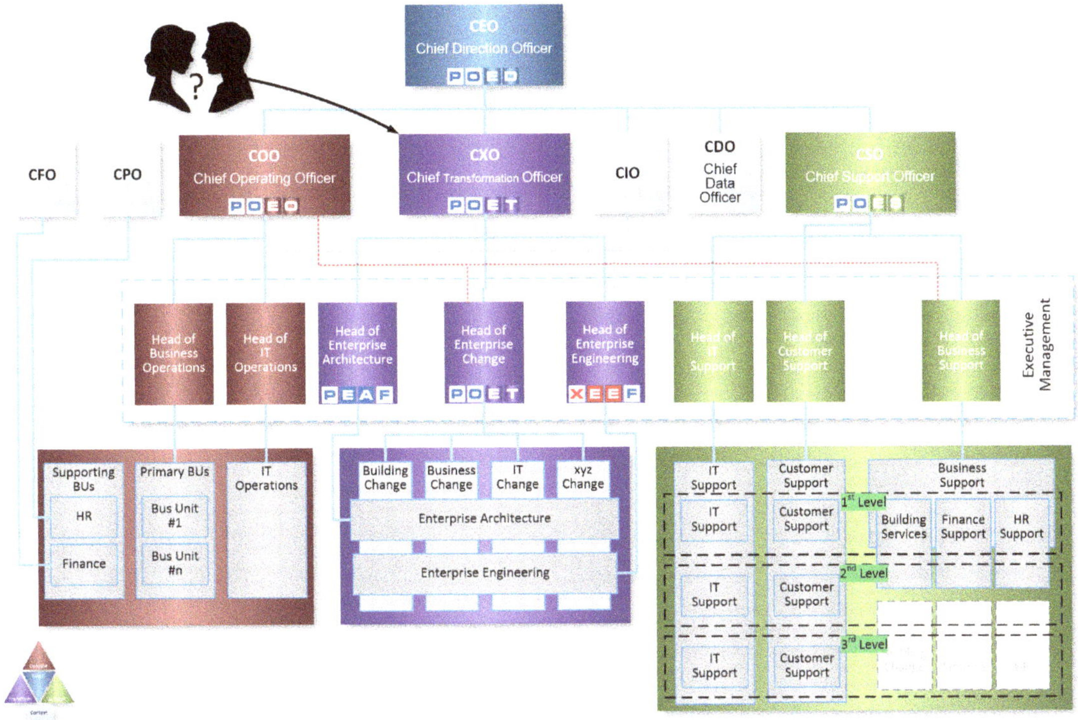

Here we suggest the Executive Structure required for an Enterprise based on DOTS.

The COO would have the Head of Business Operations and the Head of IT Operations reporting to them. To the COO, it doesn't matter if the business is being executed by a person or a machine. He is accountable for the execution of Operations, but also for the improvement to Operations. All of Operations.

Just as there is a COO (because the Operation part of the Enterprise is critical to its success), in the 21st century the same is true for the Chief Transformation Officer (CXO). There needs to be someone, at board/CxO level who is accountable for this strategically important part of the Enterprise, and to bang the boardroom table for resources to improve it. As well as the Head of Change, the CXO also has the key reports of the Transformation domain reporting to him – the Head of Enterprise Architecture and the Head of Enterprise Engineering.

The COO would have dotted line responsibility for the Head of Business Change.

The CSO would have the Heads of Business Support IT Support and Customer Support reporting to them. All support, regardless of the area will be initially handled by the same first line support and ticket issuing and managing system.

The COO would have dotted line responsibility for the Head of Enterprise Change.

The CFO and other CxO roles would be as normal with the continued representation of the CIO/CTO/IT Director role, although that role would have overseeing and dotted line responsibility to the Head of IT Operations, the Head of IT Change and the Head of IT Support.

In most Enterprises, the CXO role does not exist. This is the fundamental change that POET advocates for. Assuming the C-Suite has decided that a CXO is required, the obvious next question is "who will lead that domain?". Two possibilities exist, to either recruit from inside the Enterprise or from outside the Enterprise. In terms of outside the Enterprise, this may prove impossible or extremely difficult. When POET was first launched this role did not exist. Even today it is not in widespread use and its growth has not been steep. Where it does exist, it tends to be more of a carrot and tick role to drive Transformation forward (against any dissent) rather than a role that is accountable for improving the domain as well.

However, as time has gone on, more and more "experts" are beginning to tout this important role. For example, an article in Raconteur states:

> **"Chief transformation officer: revolutionary or functionary?**
> Some are visionaries, others project managers, the newest role in the C-suite is all about change.... it's not a job title that's been around for very long, emerging over the past decade or so as organisations realise the need to be more responsive to change"
>
> *- Raconteur (July 2018)*
> *https://bit.ly/2EGfCVk*

I would hope that they were inspired by POET – that has been around for, surprise surprise, since 2008!

If external recruitment is not an option, the alternative is internal recruitment which may turn out to be the most **Pragmatic** approach. So, if you were to appoint the role to an existing employee, who would that be?

You would probably want to choose someone who already spends an appreciable amount of time involved in Enterprise Transformation at a senior level, and since a large part of Transformation happening within Enterprises today is IT related it might seem reasonable to ask the CIO to expand his remit from just dealing with IT Transformation to dealing with Transformation as a whole. To be accountable for the Entire Transformation domain - Transforming the MAGIC used for Transformation not just its IT (which is a sub part of the Technology domain, which is a sub part of the Items domain, which is a sub part of the Enterprise Transformation domain).

The other important adjustment is to make this person accountable not only for the running of Transformation but for its improvement. This is a very very important point. Most CIO's today do not have that remit in their current role (or if they do, are rarely provided with the resources to do so) and therefore the move from CIO to CXO is not only a change from an IT focus to a Transformation focus (where IT is just one part), but also a change from one that is only accountable for running Transformation to one that also includes its improvement - The Transformation of Transformation. This will require the CXO to relinquish accountability for IT Operations and IT Support to the COO and CSO.

The COO has someone he can call on who is accountable for transforming Operations - the CXO, but the CXO has no one to call on who is accountable for transforming Transformation except himself, and he can only do that if he is given an explicit remit and mandate from the CEO to do so.

NOTE: It is not anticipated than an Enterprise would implement this, as-is. It is provided more as a suggestion to how an Enterprise may begin to organise itself differently in response to the strategic drivers of the 21st Century, namely Transformation and Support.

It is also important to consider the CDO role.

Some people refer to this as the Chief Digital Officer. **Pragmatic** refers to it as the Chief Data Officer. But Kevin, isn't that the CIO (Chief Information Officer) role? Errrrr! Maybe! Probably! Perhaps!!!

Here we are again. Because of IT's immaturity, even C level positions are confusing and contradictory from Enterprise to Enterprise.

So why don't we just use the CIO title, since Information ~ Data (We are not going to get intro some esoteric and academic conversation about data vs information vs knowledge). The problem with using the CIO title for someone to be accountable and an expert in Information/Data, is that most CIOs in the world are actually Technology focussed not Information focussed. Worse, a great proportion of those are actually Infrastructure Technology focussed.

The only thing that is clear, is that it's a mess! **Pragmatic**'s suggestion is to use the following

- CIO – Chief IT Officer
- CDO – Chief Data Officer

In the center at the bottom, we can see the high level department structure for the Transformation domain and the reporting structure. It illustrates the cross fertilisation and the dependencies of these departments.

Further depth of the Operations and Support areas is outside the scope of POET and handled in more detail in POEO and POES, however, for completeness we present their fundamental department structures here also.

KEYPOINT:

Someone should be Accountable for the strategically important Transformation capability of the Enterprise.

ADOPTION:

C-Suite: Appoint a Chief Transformation Officer (CXO).

Questions to Ponder

- Do you have a CXO?
- Who in your Enterprise will bang the boardroom table to resources to improve how Transformation is effected?
- Who in your Enterprise would be best placed to move into that role?
- Are Transformation and Support represented at the CxO level in your Enterprise?
- If not, does this cause any problems?
- What are the impact of these problems?
- What needs to happen to alleviate these problems?

The biggest enemy (or ally) of Enterprise Transformation, is Culture.

Do not underestimate the power of culture.

Do not underestimate the power of culture.

Let me just say that one more time.

Do not under-estimate the power of culture.

Culture Trumps Everything™ is much more than just a saying. It is a very cold hard fact, which if literally has the power to move mountains, or destroy Enterprises.

Bad culture trumps everything. Physics. Truth. Best Practice. Good Intentions. Good Ideas. Passion. Creativity. Teamwork. Trust. Common Sense. etc. It will take you good ideas, chew them up, spit them out, and then vilify you for having them in the first place. It takes passionate people and grinds them down until they can't remember why they were passionate about something in the first place. It destroys people's self-esteem. and like a cancer, eats away at the very core of an Enterprise.

You can have as many fantastic Methods as you like, define as many perfect Artefacts as you like and change the Items to use the most advanced technology and tools, but like a cork bobbing in the sea, they are utterly insignificant compared to the churning seas of bad Culture. Even when the sea appears calm there can be dangerous undercurrents and hidden dangers that can sink the unsinkable (as I have found from personal experience over 40 years of professional life). All Enterprises have to navigate the icebergs of culture, but many of them do not realise that they can only see 10% of the iceberg, or is it perhaps, that many of them do not want to see the iceberg, preferring to deal with the obvious 10% and ignore the hidden and cynical 90%.

Perhaps we should also introduce the term politics. Politics on the face of it should be a force for good – our countries are run by politicians after all - however, within an Enterprise, politics normally equates to a force for bad. Bad decisions are made because of politics. The more politics exists, the more bad decisions are made.

On the other hand, good culture also trumps everything. Incoherence. Lies. Worst Practice. Bad Intentions. Bad Ideas. Apathy. Stagnation. Loose Cannons. Distrust. Stupidity. etc. It enables and empowers people to achieve and be the best they can be. It can allow people, and therefore the Enterprise, to grow and blossom and to improve the products and services they provide and the lives of their Customers beyond recognition.

You can have as many bad Methods as you like, use as many awful Artefacts as you like and use the most basic of tools, but like a cork bobbing in the sea, they are utterly insignificant compared to the churning seas of good Culture.

KEYPOINT:

"Culture Trumps Everything"

-Kevin Smith

ADOPTION:

C-Suite: Instigate a review of the Culture of Transformation. Otherwise everything else is largely pointless.

Questions to Ponder

- Does Culture trump things in your Enterprise?
- Is it a power for good or ill?
- What would you change about your Enterprises Culture?
- Who is Accountable for the Culture in your Enterprise?

$$E=mc^2$$

$$\text{Enterprise Effectiveness \& Efficiency} = \text{Methods} * \text{Culture}^2$$

Einstein's famous mass-energy equivalence formula is possibly the most well-known formula of all time. It states that mass and energy are equivalent (mass and energy are never created or destroyed, they just change states), and the relationship is governed by a constant - the speed of light - squared.

Although the full implications of $E=mc^2$ don't apply to Enterprises (i.e. an Enterprise's Effectiveness and Efficiency cannot be transformed into methods, and the relationship between the two is not governed by the speed of light) it does serve as a useful way to express that an Enterprise's Effectiveness and Efficiency, while largely governed by its Methods (how it does what it does) is governed much much more by its culture - squared.

KEYPOINT:

"Culture is like the speed of light.

Very difficult to change."

- Kevin Lee Smith

ADOPTION:

C-Suite: Accept that Culture change has much more impact than changing anything else

Questions to Ponder

- Is your Enterprise as unsinkable as the Titanic?
- Do the icebergs of culture that you can see, mask the hidden dangers of the 90% that you cannot see?
- What are you doing to make sure that the 90% of culture that you cannot see, will not sink your Enterprise?

Source: NASA

Never underestimate the kind of things that a bad culture can create.

You may think there is a limit to bad culture - a point at which when the potential effects could be so catastrophic that people would pull back, but the space shuttle Challenger disaster of January 28, 1986 proves to us that the lives of seven people were naught compared with the power of culture.

The disaster resulted in a 32-month suspension in the shuttle program and the formation of the Rogers Commission, a special commission appointed by Ronald Reagan to investigate the accident. The Rogers Commission found NASA's organizational culture and decision-making processes had been key contributing factors to the accident. NASA managers had known contractor Morton Thiokol's design of the SRBs (Solid Rocket Boosters) contained a potentially catastrophic flaw in the O-rings (gas tight rubber seals between the sections of the SRBs) since 1977, but failed to address it properly. They also disregarded warnings from engineers about the dangers of launching posed by the low temperatures of that morning and had failed in adequately reporting these technical concerns to their superiors.

It is also pertinent and ironic to mention that cultural problems also surrounded the Rogers Commission itself, particularly the role of theoretical physicist Richard Feynman. His direct and apolitical style of investigating rather than following the commission schedule put him at odds with Rogers, who once commented, "Feynman is becoming a real pain".

But, even though there was an appalling disaster caused by problems deeply rooted in culture, at least the Rogers Commission and their report and recommendations would correct these failings and at last the power of culture to do massive harm would be curtailed...

Well, the power of culture is so powerful that even that was not the limit...

After another Space Shuttle disaster (Columbia in 2003), attention once again focused on the attitude of NASA management towards safety issues. The Columbia Accident Investigation Board (CAIB) concluded that NASA had failed to learn many of the lessons of Challenger. In particular, the agency had not set up a truly independent office for safety oversight; the CAIB felt that in this area, "NASA's response to the Rogers Commission did not meet the Commission's intent". The CAIB believed that "the causes of the institutional failure responsible for Challenger have not been fixed," saying that the same "flawed decision making process" that had resulted in the Challenger accident was responsible for Columbia's destruction seventeen years later.

It is pertinent to consider how ignorance is interpreted differently in the law and in business.

In the law - "Ignorance is no defence" but in business Ignorance is the "perfect defence". You can see it used on a daily basis especially for those senior people whose job it is to be accountable, claiming ignorance of knowing the bad things "workers" had been doing and promising that they will be punished. But these are not bad people.

There are no bad people, only bad environments.

Culture is the most important environment of them all and it is Management that is responsible for setting it. Good or Bad.

KEYPOINT:

Bad Culture knows no bounds.

It can destroy lives.

And Enterprises.

ADOPTION:

C-Suite: Do not underestimate the effects of bad culture.

Questions to Ponder

- What are the biggest "disasters" your Enterprise has faced?
- Did Culture play a part, and if so, what part?
- Were lessons learned or not?
- What are the top five Cultural problems facing your Enterprise?
- What would your Enterprise look and feel like if those problems were solved?
- What does your Enterprise do to improve Culture?
- Are they succeeding? Are they doing enough?

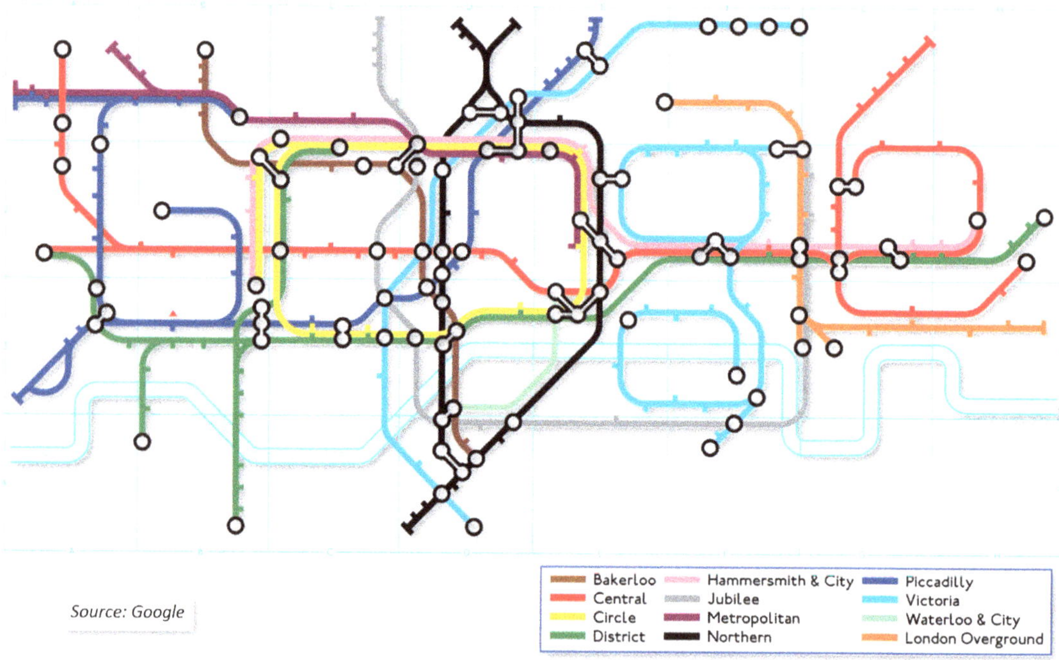

Source: Google

Never underestimate the kind of things that a good culture can create.

A small change in culture (while perhaps more difficult to achieve) can produce literally incalculable positive benefits. Culture is what delivers a Strategy, or Culture is what destroys a Strategy. Depending on the culture, it's either the oxygen of an Enterprise's success, or the cancer of Enterprise's destruction. We can define as many processes and products as we like but it's culture that will make or break them.

Do not underestimate the kind of things that a good culture can create.

You may think there is a limit to good culture - a point at which when the potential effects could be so fantastic that people would pull back, Google proves to us that there is potentially no limit to what opportunities good culture can generate. Opportunities for the Enterprise as a whole but also opportunities for the people that work at them.

While **How** an Enterprise effects the whole of Transformation is becoming a Strategic Strength or a Strategic Weakness, where massive business opportunities can be gained or massive business problems will result, the same is true of culture. An Enterprises Culture is becoming (has become?) a Strategic Strength or a Strategic Weakness, where massive business opportunities can be gained or massive business problems will result.

KEYPOINT:

Good Culture knows no bounds.

It can lift lives.

And Enterprises.

ADOPTION:

C-Suite: Do not underestimate the effects of good culture.

Questions to Ponder

- Do you think a change in Culture could produce large positive results?
- Could your Enterprise be more successful if Culture was changed?
- What changes would be necessary? How would they be carried out?
- Who is Accountable?

I think, therefore I might be...

We are all humans and in that respect we are all the same. Of course there are many differences between us but some things are fundamental and affect all of us. We love to think that we are intelligent. We are masters of the universe. We have created great art, we have created spectacles of construction, we have created electronic devices of amazing complexity and we have gone to the moon and back. Religion, philosophy etc, etc. We think we know a lot of stuff. And while our brains, can do some pretty amazing things, like anything else, like any tool, it has its weaknesses. Being human means we don't like to think about those weaknesses in our own brains. We (or rather our brains) prefer to ignore those weaknesses and instead concentrate on feeling smug!

Psychology tells us different. Psychology allows us to expose and understand these weaknesses, for until we expose and understand those weaknesses we will forever be ruled by them.

> "To err is human; to forgive, divine."
>
> ***- Alexander Pope***

Understanding and then accepting that we are a flawed species in our thinking and in our perceptions allows us to do something about those things. Those things are problems and the first step in solving any problem is to admit that it exists.

Before an alcoholic can be "saved" they must first take the most important first step and admit they are an alcoholic.

We must accept that we will make mistakes. Many many mistakes. All of us. The number of mistakes people make is not proportional to a person's standing or seniority within an Enterprise. The CEO is liable to make the same number of mistakes as the person who cleans the toilets. What is proportional is the amount of damage that a mistake that goes uncorrected can have (in general). We must therefore accept that mistakes will happen and create an environment that allows us **all** to expose and correct those mistakes without resorting to blame. The people in your Enterprise that make mistakes and correct them (including you) are your best employees. Those that make mistakes and hide them can destroy your Enterprise. "Backtracking" or performing a "U-turn" should not be met with scorn, vilification and condemnation but instead with thanks and praise.

Those that do not make mistakes are lying.

KEYPOINT:

The human brain is easily fooled.

ADOPTION:

C-Suite: Accept that we all have mental health issues. (That are largely not under our control!)

Questions to Ponder

- Do you think Psychology is important and Why?
- Do you think you make mistakes?
- What do you do when you make small mistakes?
- What do you do when you make big mistakes?
- What do others in your Enterprise do when they make small or big mistakes?
- Are people allowed to make mistakes?
- What happens to people who expose small mistakes?
- What happens to people who expose big mistakes?
- What happens to people who hide mistakes?

Source: *Washington Post*

Violinist in the Metro Station

Can you see the value when there is no price tag? In 2007 world famous violinist Joshua Bell posed as a street musician in a Washington D.C. metro station to see how many people would stop and listen. Despite the fact that he was playing a $3.5 million handcrafted violin and had just sold out a concert in Boston where ticket prices averaged $100 each, very few people stopped to appreciate his beautiful performance. He made a measly $32 that day.

Sometimes the value of something is not seen until you see it in the right context.

Seeing the value in something is not necessarily as easy as "If I spend $1,000 today I will make $10,000 tomorrow". Sometimes the most valuable things crop up in unexpected places and at unexpected times. Sometimes the most important and valuable things are not dressed in $2,000 suits from Saville Row. We need to be more open to spending the time to see the value in things that we may currently think have no value at all.

KEYPOINT:

True value is not measured by the numbers of Clicks or Likes.

ADOPTION:

C-Suite: Mandate that people Invest time to see the true value of things.

Questions to Ponder

- Do people in your Enterprise know "the cost of everything and value of nothing"?
- Do people in your Enterprise only see obvious value and miss hidden value?
- Can you think of examples where this has happened in the past?
- Who were they? What was the impact? Why do you think they acted in this way?
- What needs to change to reduce the likelihood of it happening in the future?
- Who needs to drive that change?

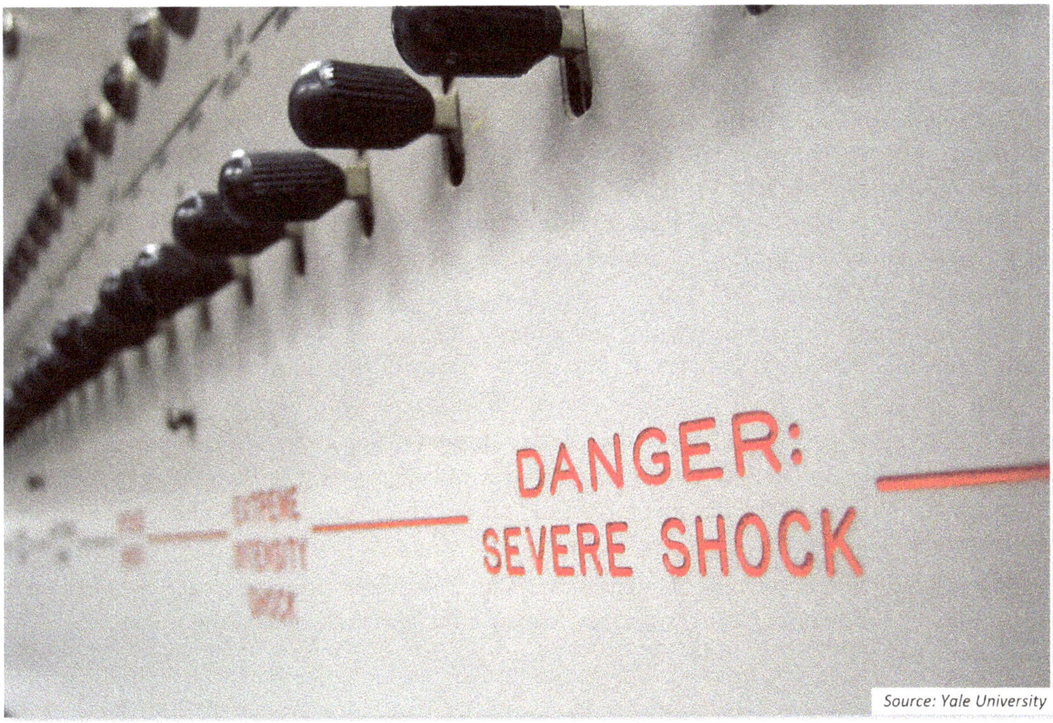

Source: Yale University

The Milgram Experiment

Humans are trained to take direction from authority figures from very early in life. An infamous experiment conducted in 1961 by Yale University psychologist Stanley Milgram, measured this willingness to obey authority figures by instructing people to perform acts that conflicted with their morals. Participants were told to play the role of "teacher" and administer electric shocks to "the learner," who was supposedly in a different room, every time they answered a question incorrectly. In reality, no one was actually being shocked. Instead, Milgram played recordings to make it sound like the learner was in a great deal of pain and wanted to end the experiment. Despite these protests, many participants continued the experiment when the authority figure urged them to, increasing the voltage after each wrong answer until some eventually administered what would be lethal electric shocks.

Authority figures are, of course, required. But to follow them blindly or to expect people to follow you blindly is deeply damaging. Of course, in general, people in authority do not knowingly ask people to do things which are damaging. We are not suggesting that people in authority knowingly tell people to do damaging things. However, this experiment shows us that people being told what to do may know something is damaging but they will continue to do it if an authority figure tells them to. It also show that the level of "authority" needs not be holding a gun to someone's head. Wearing a white coat and telling people "you must continue with the experiment" was all that was required to make most of these people electrocute other people until they were "unconscious" or possibly "dead".

Never underestimate the capacity of people to do things that they know are deeply damaging just because you are telling them to.

What is happening in many Enterprises today is akin to how the cockpits of aircraft worked many years ago. They used to be very hierarchical with the Chief Pilot almost being revered as a god who could never be questioned. Seniority was everything and seniority was always right.

Co-pilots and junior officers learned pretty fast not to question the Chief Pilot because if they did, their careers would soon be damaged.

However a number of air crashes (and their subsequent investigations) highlighted the fact that this command and control approach designed to make aircraft safe was the very thing that was crashing them. And so changes were made and the term "Cockpit Resource Management" (unfortunately the acronym is CRM!) was born. CRM's main tenet is that no person, whether, Architect, Designer, Engineer, Manager, Controller or Pilot, can perform perfectly at all times. In addition, what could be considered perfect performance in one set of circumstances might well be unacceptable in another. Therefore, people need to be seen as they really are - parts of a cooperative system.

Viewing some people or some roles as intrinsically "better" or "more correct" is worse than utterly futile, it is downright dangerous, and totally contrary to achieving the ends.

What is required, is that Enterprises begin to adopt this same CRM approach to transformation. No person, whether, Architect, Designer, Engineer or Manager can perform perfectly at all times. In addition, what could be considered perfect performance in one set of circumstances might well be unacceptable in another. Therefore, people need to be seen as they really are - parts of a cooperative system.

Viewing some people or some roles as intrinsically "better" or "more correct" is worse than utterly futile, it is downright dangerous, and totally contrary to achieving the ends.

KEYPOINT:

Sometimes the best course of action is to not do what you are being told to do.

ADOPTION:

C-Suite: Mandate that people are rewarded, not punished, for respectfully questioning authority.

Questions to Ponder

- Do people in your Enterprise do what they are told to do, rather than or what they should do?
- Can you think of examples where this has happened in the past?
- Who were they? What was the impact? Why do you think they acted in this way?
- What needs to change to reduce the likelihood of it happening in the future?
- Who needs to drive that change?

You Decide!

The Marshmallow Test

An experiment conducted in 1972 by Walter Mischel of Stanford University sought to determine if deferred gratification can be an indicator of future success.

Children, aged four to six, were taken into a room where a marshmallow was placed on the table in front of them. Before leaving each of the children alone in the room, the examiner told them they would receive a second marshmallow if the first was still on the table after 15 minutes. One-third deferred gratification long enough to receive the second marshmallow. In follow-up studies, Mischel found that those who deferred gratification were significantly more competent and received higher SAT scores than their peers, meaning that this characteristic likely remains with a person for life.

The children that went on to be more successful were the ones that didn't eat the marshmallow. They thought ahead. Thinking ahead requires us to not think so much about now. It means we are required to look into the future. To make some decisions now that will affect the future - which is, of course, one of the things that Architects are really good at.

This is especially pertinent for Enterprises, not from the point of view of future personal success but because two thirds of children sought short term benefits over long term benefits and will likely carry that into later life, especially when in later life the motivation they receives condones the behaviour. This is a cancer that afflicts 90% of all Enterprises today. These are not bad people however. They are just the product of Psychology and the context in which they work and the way that context motivates them.

KEYPOINT:

Short term gratification (quick wins) most often leads to long term failure. Delaying short term gratification, most often leads to long term success.

ADOPTION:

C-Suite: Mandate that people favour future benefits over short term gratification. If you want to pick low hanging fruit, you first have to plant a tree.

Questions to Ponder

- Do people in your Enterprise concentrate more on short term benefit rather than long term benefit?
- Can you think of examples where this has happened in the past?
- Who were they? What was the impact? Why do you think they acted in this way?
- What needs to change to reduce the likelihood of it happening in the future?
- Who needs to drive that change?

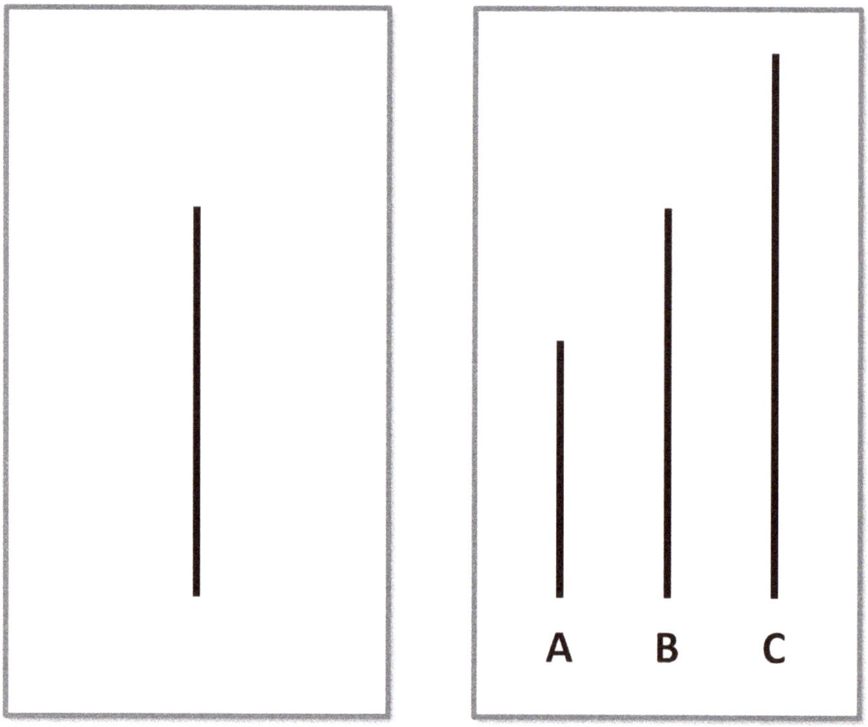

The Asch Conformity Experiment

This is a famous example of the temptation (overwhelming desire?) to conform. This series of experiments conducted in the 1950s placed one subject in a room full of actors. The person conducting the experiment held up an image with three numbered lines and asked each person in the room to identify the longest line. The actors purposely chose the incorrect line in order to determine whether the subject would answer honestly or simply go along with the group answer. The results showed that people tend to conform in group situations.

Everyone knows the tale of "The Emperor's New Clothes" by Hans Christian Andersen where it took a little child up a lamppost to point out the inconvenient truth. This can show up in Enterprises in very insidious ways. "Don't Rock the boat" or "He's a loose cannon" and similar phrases can often be used to implicitly make people conform by effectively shooting the little boy up the lamppost instead of listening to him.

KEYPOINT:

Don't be swayed by the majority.

They are wrong 80% of the time!

ADOPTION:

C-Suite: Mandate that people are rewarded, not punished, for doing the right thing, not just because it's what everyone else does/believes.

Questions to Ponder

- Do people in your Enterprise "go with the flow" rather than speaking out?
- Do people in your Enterprise thank the "little child" or vilify him?
- Can you think of examples where this has happened in the past?
- Who were they? What was the impact? Why do you think they acted in this way?
- What needs to change to reduce the likelihood of it happening in the future?
- Who needs to drive that change?

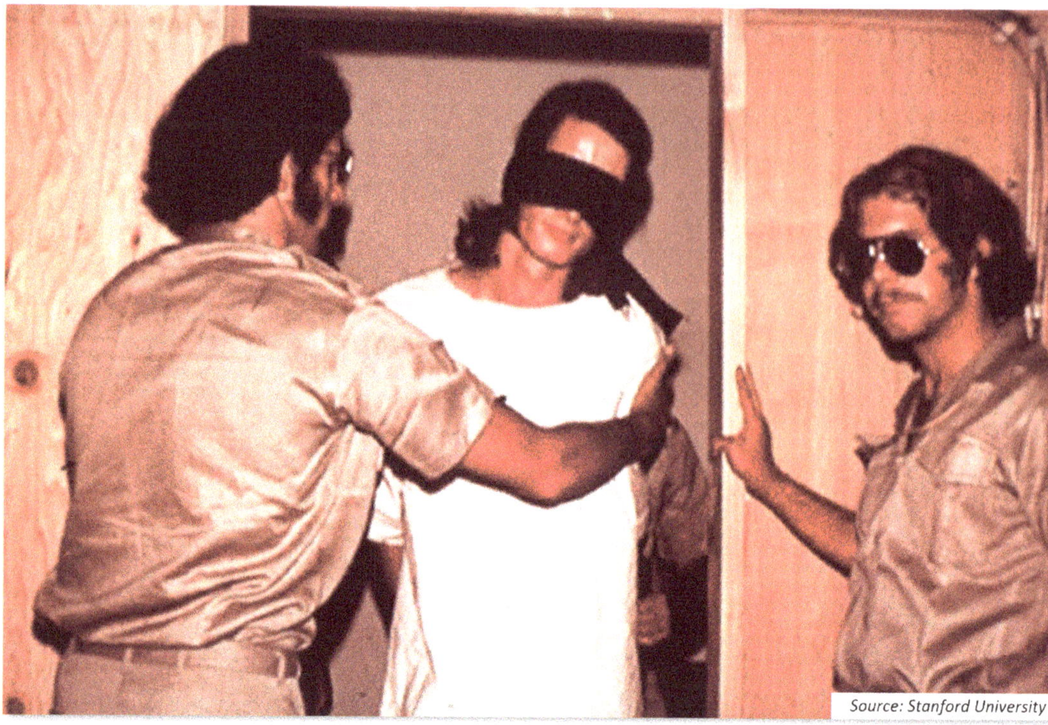
Source: Stanford University

The Stanford Prison Experiment

This infamous experiment studied the psychological effects a prison setting could have on behaviour. In 1971, a mock prison was constructed in the basement of the psychology building of Stanford University and 24 male students were randomly selected to play the role of either a prisoner or prison guard for two weeks. The students adapted to their roles a little too well, becoming aggressive to the point of inflicting psychological torture. Even psychology professor Philip Zimbardo, who acted as superintendent of the experiment, proved susceptible to its effects by allowing the abuse to continue. The study was called off after only six days due to its intensity, but it proved that situations could provoke certain behaviours, in spite of an individual's natural tendencies.

Bullying

Although outlawed in every Enterprise, bullying is still rife within Enterprises worldwide.

Bullying in this context relates to the abuse of power over rational thinking.

It is also related to forcing people to do things or work in ways that they know to be wrong or inefficient. This usually goes hand in hand with blaming the same individuals for the problems that arise.

Hiding Information / Problems

This behaviour usually occurs at management levels and prevents bad news from being transported up the food chain.

It is usually the troops on the ground that can sense things going wrong first. This is usually the first sign that a project is going wrong in some way. What can happen is that these messages can get diluted the further up the food chain they go and sometimes don't make the leap at all.

Management can feel threatened as they may not understand what the troops are telling them. Management can also feel that reporting bad news to their superiors will reflect badly on them as they are ultimately Accountable for the work carried out by the people who report to them. Having started to hide or not communicate things, it can be difficult if not impossible to then begin reporting as things get progressively worse for fear of being asked "Why didn't you report this three months ago when it first started going wrong?" a phrase that I am sure many of us have heard over the years.

> "The physics definition of power is 'The ability to do work'; many social definitions of power are more like 'The ability to **avoid** work'. Therein lie **many** practical problems..."
>
> ***- Tom Graves***

KEYPOINT:

"I hope our wisdom will grow with our power, and teach us, that the less we use our power the greater it will be."

- Thomas Jefferson.

ADOPTION:

C-Suite: Mandate that people accept that power is the ability to do work, not the ability to avoid it!

Questions to Ponder

- Do people in your Enterprise abuse power?
- Can you think of examples where this has happened in the past?
- Who were they? What was the impact? Why do you think they acted in this way?
- What needs to change to reduce the likelihood of it happening in the future?
- Who needs to drive that change?

"Never Judge a book by its cover" is a common saying. However, humans find doing that extremely difficult. We also know the saying "First impressions count", You could say the first saying is an expression of intent, while the second is an expression of reality.

Style over substance is the idea that, far from "never Judging a book by its cover", we do generally judge a lot about a book by its cover, and first impressions are indeed extremely important. As we move past first impressions, we move into the area of Style over substance where we tend to be much more impressed by how someone says something rather than what they are saying. This Style over Substance effect can also be applied to things and is heavily used in the presentation of products as well as people, using a lot of style to either detract from or cover up the substance.

A good example is Elizabeth Holmes, who burst onto the stage in 2004. Her company, Theranos, was working to develop a blood test using only a small amount of blood, which could be run in a matter of minutes rather than hours or days. By 2004 she had managed to raise six million dollars She often tried to emulate Steve Jobs, dressing in black turtleneck sweaters and speaking in a strange deep baritone voice, that sometimes slipped towards the end of interviews as she forgot and ended up talking in a normal higher pitched woman's voice. But her claims were all a sham and in June 2018, was indicted on nine counts of wire fraud and two counts of conspiracy to commit wire fraud. Prosecutors allege that she engaged in two criminal schemes, one to defraud investors, the other to defraud doctors and patients.

Style over substance favours how things look and a general feeling of happiness over anything else. It is synonymous with the outside world where celebrity and presentation has grown to outshine any fundamental value. The whole world seems consumed with how things look.

> "It's not what you say but how you say it"

This trait generally means that no one wants to rock the boat and differences of opinions and confrontations are to be avoided at all costs - regardless of the detriment to the Enterprise.

If people are mediocre, ineffective or inefficient at their jobs, then this tends to be tolerated so long as they are always happy and get on with people, smile a lot and are the "life and soul of the party" (of course there are limits but the general point stands) but if someone points this out (and by doing so annoys them) then this is not tolerated.

KEYPOINT:

"Nobody cares how much you know, until they know how much you care".

- Theodore Roosevelt

ADOPTION:

C-Suite: Mandate that people favour Substance over Style, rather than Style over Substance.

Questions to Ponder

- Do people in your Enterprise favour style over substance?
- Can you think of examples where this has happened in the past?
- Who were they? What was the impact? Why do you think they acted in this way?
- What needs to change to reduce the likelihood of it happening in the future?
- Who needs to drive that change?

© Pragmatic 365 (2008-2021)

The Halo Effect is the idea that our overall impression of a person can be based on one trait about them. However, For example, if someone has a likeable personality, people might find that person's other qualities more appealing. People may listen to them more intently, assume they are correct in what they say, allow them the benefit of the doubt, etc.

In a recent experiment, a man made two videos for a dating website. In the first video, he read the script in an upbeat manner, whereas in the second, he read the same script in a more melancholy fashion. The first video was given to a one group of girls and the second was given to another group, who watched the video in a separate room. The girls who watched the upbeat video found the man to be likeable, while the girls who watched the second video found the man to be unpleasant, even though he had read the exact same script. This can have devastating results.

For those who do not know, the picture on the left is of Jimmy Saville, who was a popular and prolific entertainer on radio and TV, in the UK, in the 60s and 70s. He also did a massive amount of fund raising, sponsorship and voluntary work. Because of his halo, people did not speak out when they had problems or worries or issues regarding him. Shortly after he died in 2011, it was discovered (or rather what was already known, was allowed to be spoken about because the halo did not protect him anymore) that he was in fact a prolific child sexual abuser. By the end of 2012, 14 police forces across the UK, were pursuing 400 lines of inquiry based on testimony from 200 witnesses. In March 2013 Her Majesty's Inspectorate of Constabulary reported that 214 of the complaints that had been made against Savile after his death would have been criminal offences if they had been reported at the time.

However, the corollary is also true, and is known as the Horn effect. If we have a negative view of someone, we are less likely to listen to them or entertain their views. We may dismiss anything they have to say as being negative and not worthy of even the time to listen to them. This can have devastating results.

For those who do not know, the picture on the right is of Stephen Christopher Yaxley-Lennon (more commonly known as Tommy Robinson) who is a person that has been vilified and character assassinated by the British News Media and Television for many years. He is always introduced by the media as "The Far Right Extremist and former leader of the EDL, Tommy Robins" instead of "Mr, Tommy Robinson". He earned this moniker because in 2009 he started an organisation called the English Defence League (EDL) after he had read a newspaper article about local Islamists attempting to recruit men outside a bakery in Luton to fight for the Taliban in Afghanistan. Unfortunately, the (real) far right infiltrated the EDL and turned it into a racist organisation. Because of this, he left it and cut off all ties to it in 2013, but note that despite this, he is still introduced as "The former leader of the EDL". It's interesting how the media cling on to that association even though he disassociated himself from them many years ago. The horns that were given to him from 2009 have continued to be attached even though he clearly states he is not racist (because Islam is not a race, it is a religion) but he believes there are teachings in Islam that are counter to English life, citing such things as death for homosexuals and apostates, and the suppression of women in society.

KEYPOINT:

"It's hard to see a halo when you're looking for horns."

- Cullen Hightower

ADOPTION:

C-Suite: Initiate a review of people who have been given Halos or Horns.

Questions to Ponder

- Do people in your Enterprise wear halos?
- Who were they? What was the impact?
- What needs to change to reduce the likelihood of it happening in the future?
- Do people in your Enterprise wear horns?
- Who were they? What was the impact?
- What needs to change to reduce the likelihood of it happening in the future?
- Who needs to drive these changes?

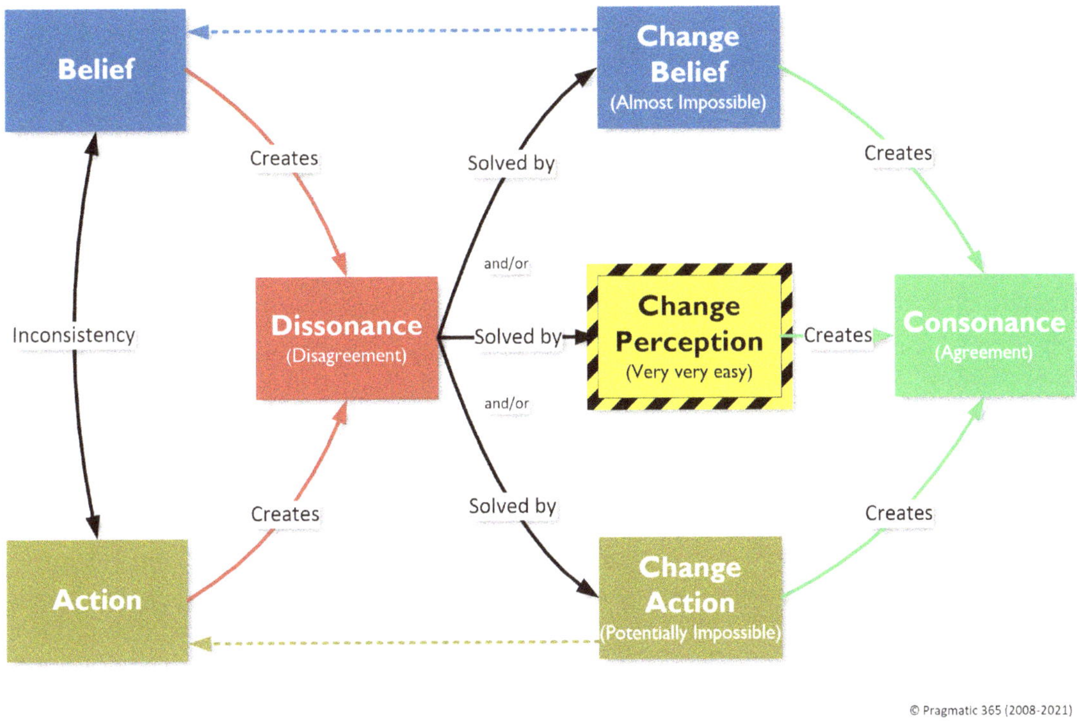

Cognitive dissonance theory is based on three fundamental assumptions:

- Humans are sensitive to inconsistencies between actions and beliefs.
- Recognition of this inconsistency will cause dissonance, and will motivate an individual to resolve the dissonance.
- Dissonance will be resolved in one of three basic ways:

	Belief	Action	Perception
1	Change	Preserve	Preserve
2	Preserve	Change	Preserve
3	Preserve	Preserve	Change

Changing ones beliefs is very hard and this very rarely happens. Changing one's actions is generally not possible - only future actions can be changed and therefore while discussions and arguments about whether the action was right or wrong can occur they are largely immaterial. Because of these two things, the dissonance (more often than not) causes the person to change their perceptions in order to justify their actions and amazingly people can change their perceptions quite easily - by lying to ourselves. Convincingly.

It's mankind's greatest achievement!

Changing one's perceptions changes the way you view/remember/perceive your action - in other words you "rationalize" your actions. For example, you might decide that the test you cheated on was for a dumb class that you didn't need anyway. Or you may say to yourself that everyone cheats so why not you. In other words, you think about your action in a different manner or context so that it no longer appears to be inconsistent with your beliefs.

In relation to Enterprises, it is not so much actions, but decisions - the decision is the action - and while an action that has occurred cannot be changed, a decision that has occurred can. However, as humans we are so used to changing our perceptions (lying to ourselves) that even though decisions can be changed we can easily fall into the routine of justifying our decisions instead of changing them.

For a decision to be changed, there first has to be a change in the context or implications or culture that was used to make that decision. That might mean the exposure and acceptance of new information, or the acceptance of information that did exist before but was not taken into account, or a change in culture.

It is often felt that there are two types of people; "Bad People" - those who know their decision to be "wrong" and use any means (including but limited to lying to themselves) to preserve it; and "Good People" - those who find out their decision was "wrong". But what makes a decision "wrong"? Who is to say what is "right" and what is "wrong"? This is where culture plays a massive part.

All people tend to be generally logical (not the same as moral) and really quite simple in the way they think (including me - and you!). Tell someone that acting strategically is monumentally important but reward them with money for acting tactically and guess what they are likely to do? There are no bad people. Only bad information and bad culture. Everything else is smoke and mirrors (created by bad culture!).

Cultural aspects never (explicitly) come into making decisions or evaluating why decisions were taken but it is exactly these cultural aspects that are the most powerful.

The effects of Cognitive dissonance can be many and varied and usually range from very bad to catastrophic. For example, incorrect decisions do not get corrected, people get demotivated and disengaged, etc.

Cognitive Dissonance is described as when someone holds two or more contradicting beliefs, ideas or values. Interestingly this is exactly what Architects do all the time and is probably what they are best at doing! Keeping conflicting beliefs or ideas in your head creates possibilities. In fact they hold intricate and complex networks of possibilities in their heads. When facts come to light or decisions are made some possibilities close down - this has a knock on effect that ripples through the remaining possibilities. Don't ask me how my brain does that - I have no idea - but that's probably a good thing!

KEYPOINT:

"How often it is that the angry man rages denial, of what his inner self is telling him."

- Frank Herbert (Dune)

ADOPTION:

C-Suite: Mandate that people recognise Cognitive Dissonance, and they don't lie to themselves.

Questions to Ponder

- Do people in your Enterprise lie to themselves?
- Do you lie tro yourself? Convincingly?
- Can you think of examples where this has happened in the past?
- Who were they? What was the impact? Why do you think they acted in this way?
- What needs to change to reduce the likelihood of it happening in the future?
- Who needs to drive that change?

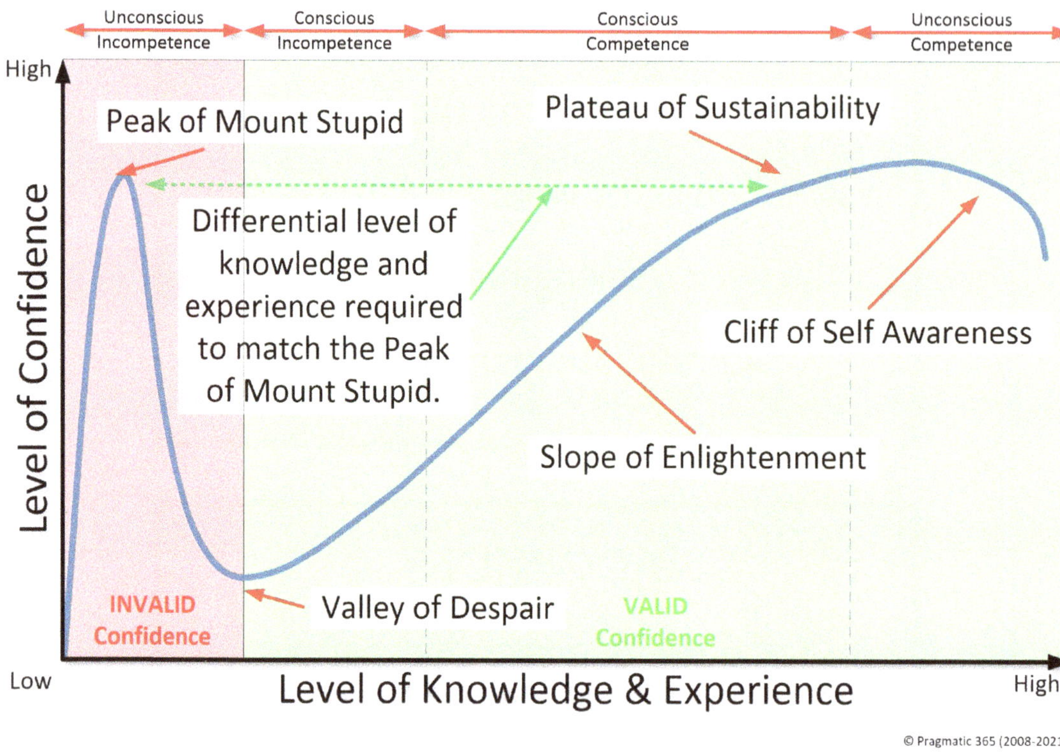

The Dunning-Kruger effect (defined by David Dunning & Justin Kruger) is a cognitive bias, where people that have a low Competence tend to have the illusion of superiority, as they do not possess the ability to assess their own ability. This means they assess their own ability as higher than it actually is. Essentially, the lack of people with low-cognitive ability, to recognise they are of low-cognitive ability - because they do not possess the cognitive ability, to assess their cognitive ability.

The less people know, the less they realise that there are things they don't know.

The more people know, the more they realise that there are things they don't know.

There is a saying:

> "If you think you understand the problem, you clearly do not understand the problem."
>
> *- Unknown*

The red area denotes those that have "Invalid" confidence. That is, their confidence largely outweighs their level of knowledge and experience. People in this area are often outspoken and passionate about what they believe, largely because they think they know everything there is to know.

A good example would be Alexandria Ocasio-Cortez, whose passion and commitment to what she says cannot be underestimated, but what she says is often confused or just plain wrong.

For example, she thinks that the unemployment rate in the USA is low because...

> "most people have two jobs."
>
> ***- Alexandria Ocasio-Cortez***

She was also happy that Amazon decided to pull out of creating a new facility in New York City (producing 25,000 jobs plus thousands of secondary jobs that would have been created such as restaurants etc) because New York could...

> "spend the $3 billion tax incentives on other things."
>
> ***- Alexandria Ocasio-Cortez***

Please bear in mind she graduated cum laude (with honour) from Boston University's College of Arts and Sciences in 2011, majoring in international relations and economics.

The green area denotes those that have "Valid" confidence, in that their confidence broadly matches their level of knowledge and experience. Notice that people in this area need to accumulate a significant level of knowledge and experience, to be able to match the level of confidence of people on Peak of Mount Stupid. This discrepancy can, of course, therefore cause massive problems that must be identified if they are to be dealt with effectively.

The one thing you need to be careful about is assuming that the Dunning-Kruger effect says how stupid people are. It is more about how people struggle to evaluate themselves accurately because if they are good at a task, they can see their mistakes clearly, and if they aren't good at a task, they can't see their mistakes at all. So, it is more about specific abilities than overall intelligence. {{Amber Smith}}

It should also be noted that in the original work, they noted that there was an inverse effect in the upper quadrant of those interviewed - namely, that experts who had passed the area of conscious competence and into the region you identify as the plateau of sustainability, there is often a drop in confidence as these experts tend to assess their knowledge, not against their peers, but against the knowledge they have and are aware that they don't have - often expressed as "the more I learn, the less I know" – the Cliff of Self Awareness. Thus, Dunning-Kruger also demonstrated that the more one learns, the more one becomes a master or guru - the lower they score on a self-assessment. Thus, in fact, only those in the centre - the "professional practitioners" who are consciously competent tend to be the only members who do self-assess accurately (within the usual range of error). {{Taiss Quartapa}}

KEYPOINT:

Those who are Unconsciously Incompetent, are the one's most passionate that they are right!

ADOPTION:

C-Suite: Mandate that passion is no substitute for evidence.

Questions to Ponder

- Do people in your Enterprise exhibit high levels of confidence, while having a low level of knowledge and/or experience?
- Can you think of examples where this has happened in the past?
- Who were they? What was the impact? Why do you think they acted in this way?
- What needs to change to reduce the likelihood of it happening in the future?
- Who needs to drive that change?

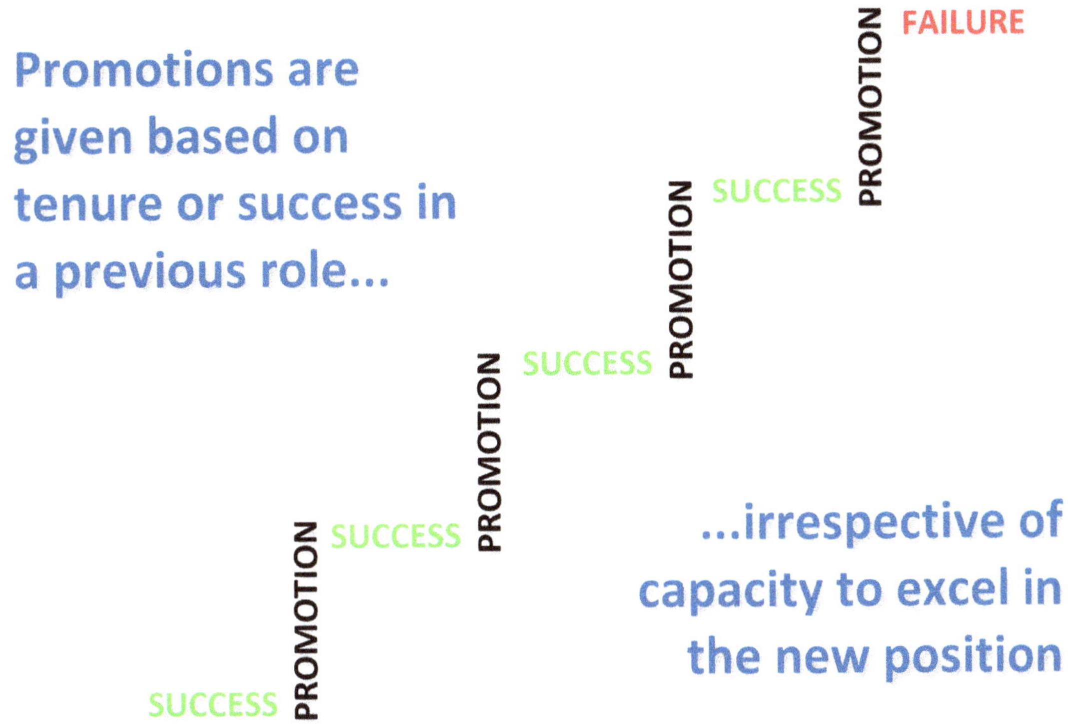

The Peter Principle (developed by Laurence J Peter and published by William Morrow and Company in 1969) says that people in any hierarchy tend to rise to their "level of incompetence", because the skills required to make someone good in one job, are not necessarily the skills required for another job. For example, a good engineer would probably be a bad manager, and a good manager would probably be a bad engineer.

I had never heard the name "The Peter Principle" but very quickly after starting work in 1980, I heard a saying: "People tend to be promoted to their level of incompetence". Very soon afterwards (and throughout a professional career spanning 40 years) I have seen it happen with my own eyes.

In 2018, professors Alan Benson, Danielle Li, and Kelly Shue analyzed sales workers' performance and promotion practices at 214 American businesses to test the veracity of the Peter principle. They found that these companies tended to promote employees to management position based on their performance in their previous position, rather than based on managerial potential. Consistent with the Peter principle, the researchers found that high performing sales employees were likelier to be promoted, and that they were likelier to perform poorly as managers, leading to considerable costs to the businesses.[1]

[1] - *Benson, Alan; Li, Danielle; Shue, Kelly (February 2018). "Promotions and the Peter Principle". NBER Working Paper. **24343**: 1–54. doi:10.3386/w24343. Retrieved May 22, 2018.*

KEYPOINT:

Success should not be promoted.

ADOPTION:

C-Suite: Mandate that promotions and recruitment should be based on the ability to do the promoted job, not on the success in a previous job.

Questions to Ponder

- Do people in your Enterprise promote based on success in a previous role, or the capacity to excel in the new role?
- Can you think of examples where this has happened in the past?
- Who were they? What was the impact? Why do you think they acted in this way?
- What needs to change to reduce the likelihood of it happening in the future?
- Who needs to drive that change?

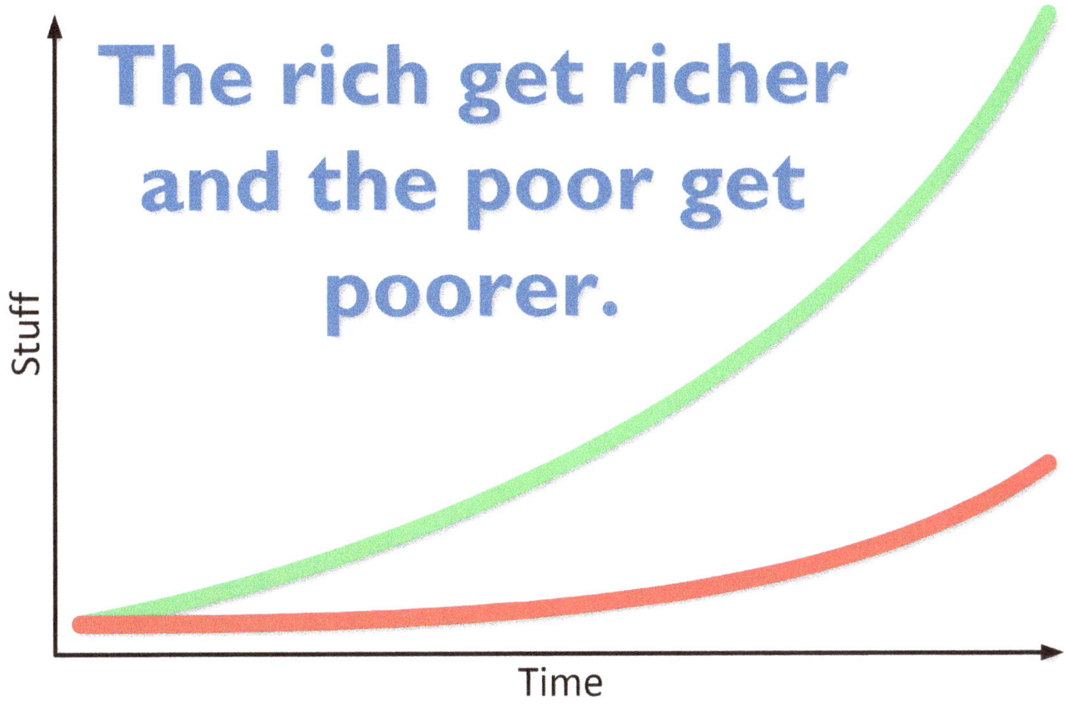

The Matthew Effect (principle, law) is social phenomenon whereby those who have, get more and those who have not get less. It appears to be a universal truth which applies to almost anything, and while the output of its effects are clear, its cause can be less so. Whenever inequality happens, one school of thought says that it is because one group is oppressing the other group. This group tends to view everything through the simplistic prison of oppressors and the oppressed. To them, the reasons for something happening is always because some one or group has decided to oppress and exploit another group. While this thinking is virtuous, it has a fundamental obvious flaw in that sometimes the reasons things happen is not because one person or group is oppressing another, but because of natural laws of nature.

The theologians of you will no doubt know that the name of the phenomenon comes from the two parables of Jesus in the Synoptic Gospels.

The concept concludes both synoptic versions of the parable of the talents:

> "For to every one who has will more be given, and he will have abundance; but from him who has not, even what he has will be taken away."
>
> —***Matthew 25:29, RSV.***

> "I tell you, that to every one who has will more be given; but from him who has not, even what he has will be taken away."
>
> —***Luke 19:26, RSV.***

The concept concludes two of the three synoptic versions of the parable of the lamp under a bushel (absent in the version of Matthew):

> "For to him who has will more be given; and from him who has not, even what he has will be taken away"

—***Mark 4:25, RSV.***

> "Take heed then how you hear; for to him who has will more be given, and from him who has not, even what he thinks that he has will be taken away."

—***Luke 8:18, RSV.***

The concept is presented again in Matthew outside of a parable during Christ's explanation to his disciples of the purpose of parables:

> "And he answered them, "To you it has been given to know the secrets of the kingdom of heaven, but to them it has not been given. For to him who has will more be given, and he will have abundance; but from him who has not, even what he has will be taken away."

—***Matthew 13:11–12, RSV.***

But what has all this got to do with the Transformation of Enterprises? Simply that an Enterprise should be wary when bestowing accolades, awards and promotions, as those that receive them, because they have received them, are likely to receive more of them, not because they deserve them.

It should also be noted that the corollary is also true. An Enterprise should be wary when disciplining, criticising, and negatively viewing employees, as those that receive them, because they have received them, are likely to receive more of them, not because they deserve them.

> KEYPOINT:
>
> Do not let the past, unduly affect the future.

> ADOPTION:
>
> C-Suite: Mandate that those receiving acolades or critism should not receive them because of previous accolades or criticism.

Questions to Ponder

- Do people in your Enterprise who receive praise and accoldaes, seem to be getting more of their fair share?
- Do people in your Enterprise who receive criticism and discipline, seem to be getting more of their fair share?
- Can you think of examples where this has happened in the past?
- Who were they? What was the impact? Why do you think they acted in this way?
- What needs to change to reduce the likelihood of it happening in the future?
- Who needs to drive that change?

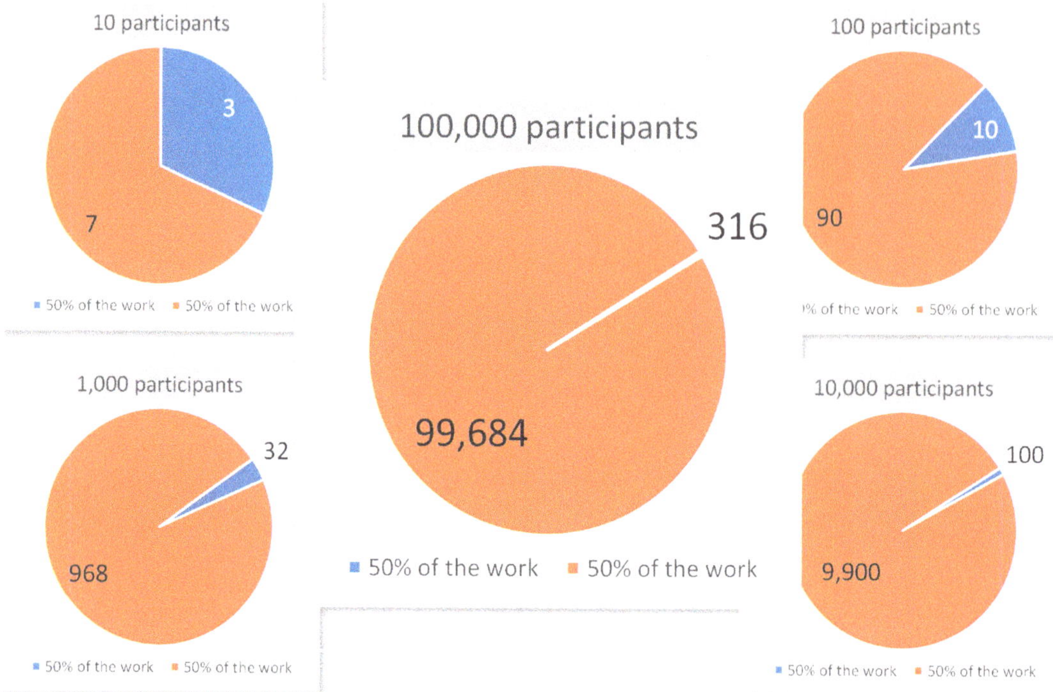

Price's law (named after Derek J. de Solla Price, England (1922-1983), referred to the relationship between the literature on a subject and the number of authors in the subject area. He found/stated that half of the publications come from the square root of all contributors. This phenomenon has since been show to be much more ubiquitous, in that it applies to just about any endeavour, meaning that more generally 50% of the participants in any endeavour are made up of the square root of the total number of participants.

What does this mean for Enterprises? If you are the owner or manager of any substantially sizes Enterprise, the ratio of one 50% to the other 50% can be extremely high. This has implications not only for the owners of the Enterprise as a whole, but equally importantly for the larger 50% of the workforce.

In this ultimate example here, we find that 316 people contribute to 50% of the work being done. So, these 316 people are ultra-important. But not because we should adore them. They are important because if the Enterprise loses even a small number of these people, it will be extremely difficult to replace them.

You might say that this small 50% group are obviously the executives and senior management. I would say that's dead wrong. In my experience, most Enterprise could lose 50% of their managers and rather than having detrimental effect on the Enterprise, would many times have a positive effect! I think that is borne out by many example of Enterprise that have culled the management.

This means if you happened to lose 0.1% of the people but that 0.1% was the wrong 0.1%, you would lose 15% of the work being done by the Enterprise!

So, in this example, losing the wrong 100 people could destroy the Enterprise.

KEYPOINT:

Competence grows linearly.

Incompetence grows exponentially.

ADOPTION:

C-Suite: When assessing value, bear in mind Price's Law.

Questions to Ponder

- How many employees does your Enterprise have?
- What is the square root of that value?
- In your enterprise, who are the people that create the most value?
- Are the other people somehow not useful?
- What puts some people in one group or the other?

NOTE – This "problem" with culture is linked to Style Over Substance and the Dunning-Kruger Effect defined elsewhere.

If you ask people "What are the skills are required for someone to be an effective and efficient manager?" you would get a list something like this:

- Good Communication Skills.
- Ability to Delegate.
- Think Strategically.
- Empower the Team.
- Trustworthy.
- Listening to and respect for Others.
- Discipline and Focus.
- Being Organised.
- Good Time Management.
- Reliable.
- Gets Results.

Over a 40 year career, I have known many many many managers and many many many people who were not managers but aspired to be. I would also say that in my experience, at least 70% of the people who were managers, were really bad at being managers, displaying almost none of the skills associated with good managers and in many cases exactly the opposite (for example not looking at the bigger picture, not respecting and listening to other peoples opinions, not delegating but micromanaging, etc). I would also say that at least 70% or more of people who were not managers (but would like to have been), would have made excellent managers, as they displayed almost all the skills of good managers (e.g looking at the bigger picture, respecting and listening to other people's opinions, not looking to micromanage others, etc).

So what the hell is going on here?

I believe the problem is related to Sociopathy and the traits of Sociopaths.

Of course, I am no psychology expert, so what I say is not based on sound scientific evidence, however, it is based on 40 years of in the field observations and a mind that can spot patterns.

Some of the major traits of Sociopaths are the following:

- Amenable
- Likeable
- Persuasive
- Charming
- Manipulative
- Cunning
- Grandiose Sense of Self
- Pathological Lying
- Lack of remorse, shame or guilt
- Shallow emotions
- Callousness/Lack of Empathy

Research into the kinds of jobs that Sociopaths are interested show time and time again that the first place on the list goes to Capitalist positions of leadership (Managers, CxO's, etc) offer power, autonomy, command, and status.

These traits largely affect how one person can manipulate other people. For example, for a Manager, whether it is people below them (report to them), on the same level (other managers) or above them (CxOs).

It is also very difficult for people to separate the charming, amenable, likeable and charming traits of someone from other, perhaps more valid traits – aka traits more specific to a particular job.

Until Enterprises recognise this as a serious problem which can cause other and numerous knock-on problems, we will continue to have people rising to positions of power that are exactly the opposite of the people that we need in those positions.

KEYPOINT:

"The trouble with Sociopaths, is that they are very, very nice people!"

- Kevin Lee Smith

ADOPTION:

C-Suite: Recognise that the traits required to gain promotion, are no necessarily the traits required to execute the job.

Questions to Ponder

- Are there any Sociopaths in your Enterprise?
- Have you seen any sociopathic traits?
- Who were they? What was the impact? Why do you think they acted in this way?
- What needs to change to reduce the likelihood of it happening in the future?
- Who needs to drive that change?

Belbin

Myers Briggs

Abstract or Concrete?	Temperament Cooperative or Utilitarian?	Role Directive or Informative?	Role Variant Expressive or Attentive ?
Introspective (N)	Idealist (NF) *Diplomatic*	Mentor (NFJ) *Developing*	Teacher (ENFJ): *Educating*
			Counselor (INFJ): *Guiding*
		Advocate (NFP) *Mediating*	Champion (ENFP): *Motivating*
			Healer (INFP): *Conciliating*
	Rational (NT) *Strategic*	Coordinator (NTJ) *Arranging*	Fieldmarshal (ENTJ): *Mobilizing*
			Mastermind (INTJ): *Entailing*
		Engineer (NTP) *Constructing*	Inventor (ENTP): *Devising*
			Architect (INTP): *Designing*
Observant (S)	Guardian (SJ) *Logistical*	Administrator (STJ) *Regulating*	Supervisor (ESTJ): *Enforcing*
			Inspector (ISTJ): *Certifying*
		Conservator (SFJ) *Supporting*	Provider (ESFJ): *Supplying*
			Protector (ISFJ): *Securing*
	Artisan (SP) *Tactical*	Operator (STP) *Expediting*	Promoter (ESTP): *Persuading*
			Crafter (ISTP): *Instrumenting*
		Entertainer (SFP) *Improvising*	Performer (ESFP): *Demonstrating*
			Composer (ISFP): *Synthesizing*

Although we all like to think of ourselves as individuals (and that's a good thing) it is possible to create categories or "types" of people traits, based on certain criteria. Having created these categories, it is then possible to compare and contrast these traits to understand how one person relates to (or should relate to?) another person.

This is a bit of a minefield though, as you will find proponents and detractors alike that hold very firmly held beliefs about the accuracy or otherwise of such methods. Personally, I think they are wonderful methods for understanding yourself, other people, how you interact with other people and how other people interact with you. Anything that makes understanding and communication better, and easier has got to be a good idea!

People test their own personality traits using these links

- www.16personalities.com
- www.123test.com

The Belbin website is www.belbin.com and the MBTI one is www.myersbriggs.org

Highlighted in red are the categories I fall into for Belbin and MBTI.

In Belbin I am categorised as a plant and a shaper, while in MBTI I am categorised as a Mastermind and an Architect.

The reason I fall into two categories, is because for some people they are truly a merging of two distinct but related types. For example, I have long thought of myself as an architect and an engineer. Two roles that are fundamentally different, and yet could be considered to be two sides of the same coin.

KEYPOINT:

People with different personality traits are required for different roles

ADOPTION:

C-Suite: Initiate an evaluation of everyone's personality traits vs the traits required to do their job.

Questions to Ponder

- What are your MBTI or Belbin results?
- Do you agree with them?
- What are the MBTI or Belbin results of your colleagues?
- Does your Enterprise use personality trait measurement?
- If not, do you think it would be beneficial?

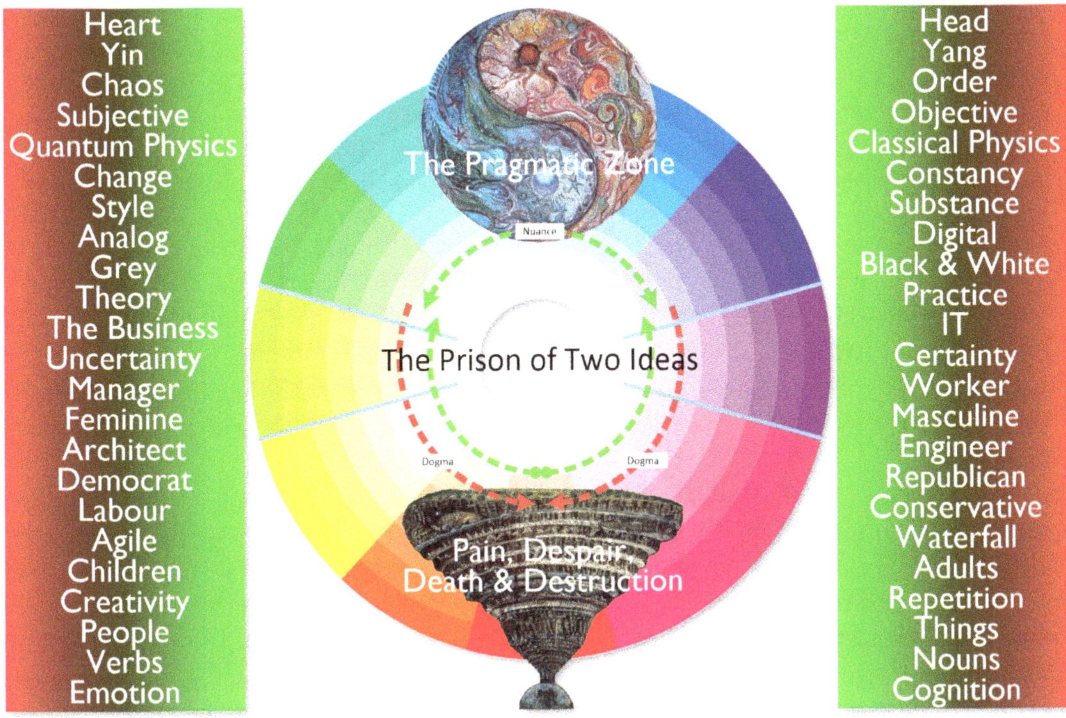

First of all, I need to make something very very clear.

Chaos is not inherently bad, and Order is not inherently good. Both have the capacity for good and bad. Whoever thought of those names initially made a big big mistake because in most civilisations, the connotations are that chaos is bad and order is good, which spikes any conversation from the get-go. So let's put those connotations in a box right at the start.

What we can say (because history teaches us) is that 100% Chaos is inherently bad and 100% Order is inherently bad. So, it is plainly obvious that a mixture is required.

You may think of that as a kind of battle where one "wins" out over the other, and in a way this is true, but this mixture happens, not by one overruling the other so to speak, but by one inhibiting or limiting the other more than the other inhibits them. So one "wins" by taking away from the other. Amazingly this is exactly what very intelligent people now say about the left-brain right-brain debate. It is now said that each hemisphere is actually the same, containing both left brain and right brain features in old money. One hemisphere "wins out" over the other by disabling parts in the other hemisphere.

One interesting thing I have observed though is that, one trait of the "left" is feeling an accomplishment when they have caused the other to fail rather when they have succeeded, while an observed trait of the "right" is a feeling of accomplishment when they have succeeded, rather when the other has failed.

So, with the good/bad connotations put firmly in the bottom of a locked filing cabinet stuck in a disused lavatory with a sign on the door saying "Beware of the Leopard.", *(ref. Douglas Adams)* we can move on.

I am not going to spout the usual stuff about Taoism and Chaos Theory. Much more has already been written by much better people than me.

But I am going to speak about is the patterns of chaos and order I have, without my awareness, observed over 40 years or so, and have only just coalesced in my mind and come forward from my subconscious to my conscious mind..

We can slice and dice people and Enterprises into many groups and subgroups, some overlapping, some not, but I have realised a correlation between the items I list on the left and which I list on the right. It is common for people (because we are all individuals) to sit in camps that are on the left and the right. For example, it is quite likely to find a business worker who is a woman, trained in Engineering, that votes Democrat in the US (Labour in the UK), who thinks like and adult and prefers agile over waterfall. It is also quite likely we could find an IT manager, who is a man, trained in architecture, that votes Republican in the US (Conservative in the UK) who thinks like a child and prefers waterfall to agile. And of course, many permutations in between.

Having said all that, I have personally witnessed a general trend that forms these two groups, so while there are exceptions at either end of the bell curve, there is a pronounced alignment in the middle.

Why am I prattling on about all this? Because in order for groups of people to work together harmoniously and productively they need to understand each other and understanding each other is fundamentally about understanding how the other side thinks. I would also say, "and why", but I am not sure why they think the way they do is important. They do, you will not change them and so the best we can achieve is understand them.

As we move further clockwise, our views become more extreme and our thoughts become more entrenched. If this continues, we stray into "The Prison of Two Ideas" *(ref. Greg Gutfeld)*. This is where both sides are held captive by their own views and actively dismiss anything that does not conform to their current beliefs. This is a precipice. A Precipice that the US political world is currently standing on (as of April October). Many Enterprises are also standing on this precipice.

Ultimately both sides taken to the extreme usually results in large numbers of people dying. (e.g Stalin or Hitler).

Once we have entered "The Prison of Two Ideas" it is extremely difficult to move back to the centre without a lot of pain. Whatever direction you take, it results in more pain, either to your opponent or to you. And since humans tend to always choose the least painful option, the most likely outcome is a further descent towards Pain, Despair, Death and Destruction. However, a return to the centre may be so painful that a descent into the abys is required, at which point, it doesn't really matter what you do because either route will be less painful.

There is certainly conflict between each of the pairs listed and is often spoke of in terms of X vs Y. E.g. Management vs Workers, Business vs IT, Architects vs Engineers, Agile vs Waterfall. For an Enterprise to increase effectiveness and efficiency in anything, these conflicts need to be exposed, understood, and accommodated. Or is that my Order side telling me to apply order to the problem when in fact, applying Chaos is the solution? Perhaps applying both is the key!

Either way, a descent into the abys helps no one.

KEYPOINT:

"In all chaos, there is a cosmos.

In all disorder, a secret order."

- Carl Jung

ADOPTION:

C-Suite: Mandate that people seek to balance Chaos with Order. Never to remove Chaos or Order.

Questions to Ponder

- Where do you fit into this diagram?
- Does it change if you consider professional vs private life?
- Does it change upon situations? If you are angry or calm?
- Can you think of examples of your yin and examples of your yang?
- Does change always bring chaos into order, or can it also bring order into chaos?
- Which areas of your Enterprise have a good balance of chaos and order?
- Which areas have too much chaos?
- Which areas have too much order?

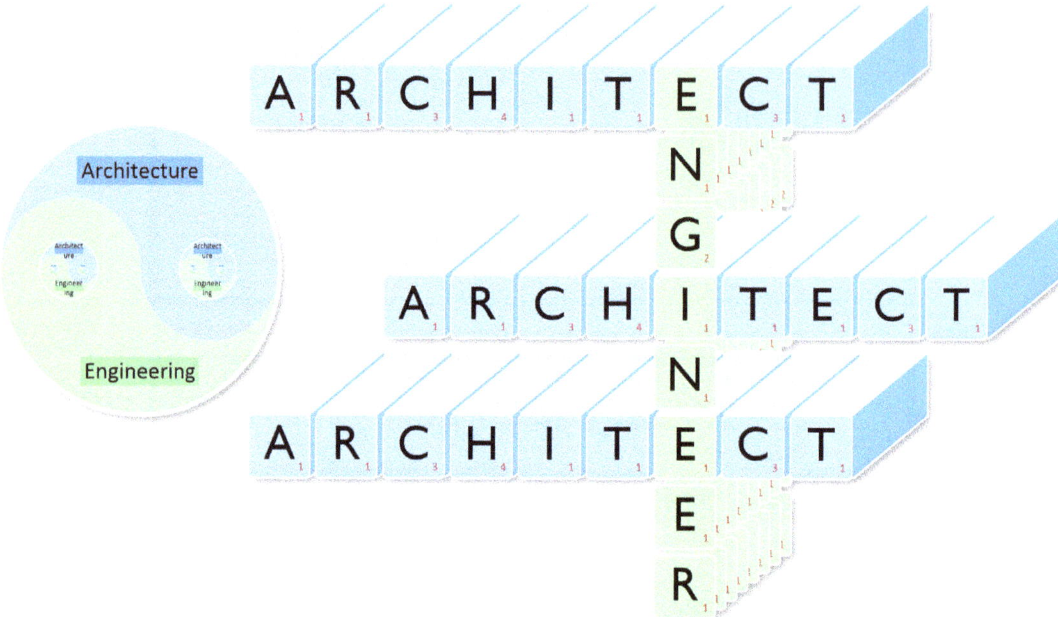

It seems everyone these days works on solutions. Thinking about one solution or another, solving problems, discussing or arguing with others on which is the right solution or not. People tend to concentrate on solutions because a solution to a problem is the end goal. There is also a psychological aspect to it - whoever's solution is adopted proves their solution was superior (supposedly - in my experience that's not always the case!).

It is human nature to answer questions - to create solutions.

Of course. The Architecture Paradigm™ is also about providing solutions and dealing with their complexity, but the approach focusses much more on understanding the problem - for when you truly understand a problem, solutions tend to be:

a) much easier to see and
b) much more effective and efficient.

However, The Architecture Paradigm™ also recognises that the approach must integrate with work that is to come later, namely Engineering.

Architecting is more concerned with WHY we need a solution which largely involves asking questions and understanding things. Engineering is more concerned with HOW the solution will be made real which largely involves creating solutions and talking.

It could be said that Architecting and Engineering are two sides of the same coin.

KEYPOINT:

Architecture and Engineering are two sides of the same coin.

ADOPTION:

C-Suite: Train Architects to understand Engineers. Train Engineers to understand Architects. Train Management to undertstand both.

Questions to Ponder

- Do the Management in your Enterprise, know the difference between Architecture and Engineering?
- Do the Workers in your Enterprise, know the difference between Architecture and Engineering?
- Does your Enterprise use Architecture and Engineering appropriately?
- If not, what problems are created?

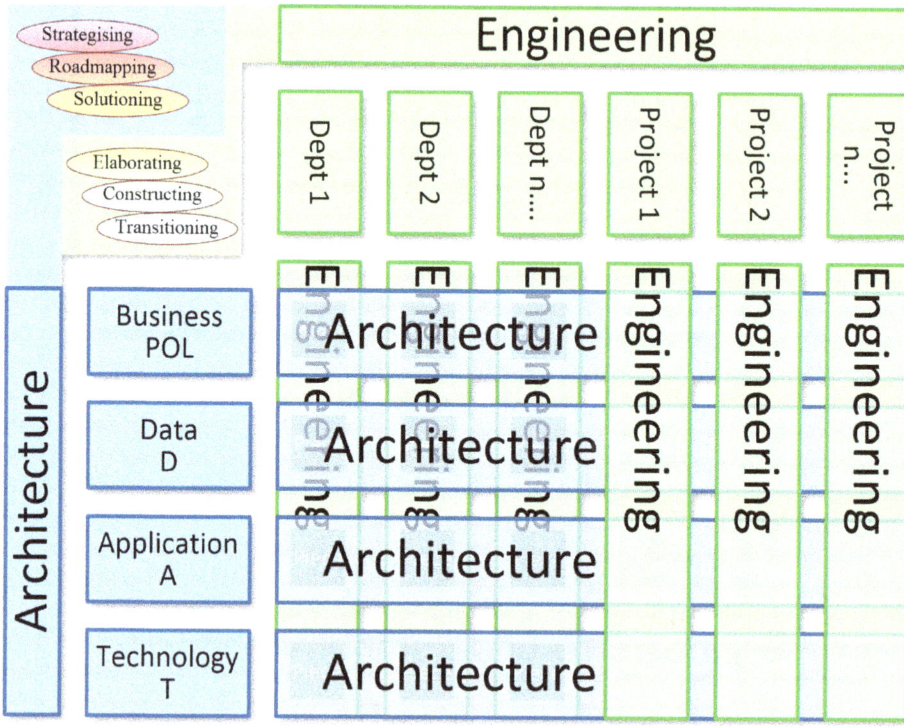

A fundamental confusion that people have when people try to explain or advocate the Architecture of something, is that just because an Architect is talking about the **whole**, it does not mean they are advocating building the whole, or building the whole immediately. By definition, Architecture (**fundamentals)** are **high level**, and by definition, the **whole** is **big**. Comments such as

> "Yes that's all very good but it's all **high level**, and it's just **too big**, we can't do it all (in a short space of time), so we won't do anything at all"

illustrates that confusion. Architecture, by definition, is **high level** and is **big.** So, the next time someone says that something Architectural is "**high level** and **big**" as a means to dismiss it, you should say…

> "Yes, it is! If it were not high level and big, it wouldn't be Architecture!
> And it is precisely because it is high level and big, that it is important."

When we say Architect horizontally, it means that Architecture tends to (should) consider the fundamental structure of something large and complex (If it were not large or complex there is little need for Architecture) and for that you have to (should) consider the whole. We also say horizontally because Architecture tends to (should) layer things and is concerned with systemic qualities and capabilities such as Process, Organisation or Locatgion – as a whole, or Data – as a whole, or Applications – as a whole, or Technology – as whole.

Because Architecture tends to (should) consider things from a Contextual and/or Conceptual and/or Logical perspectives this allows us to consider the whole.

The phases mostly concerned with Architecture work are during the Strategising, Roadmapping and Solutioning phases of Transformation.

Whenever we perform Architecture work (Business Architecture, Enterprise/Transformation Architecture, Solution Architecture, Application Architecture, Data Architecture, Infrastructure Architecture, etc) we MUST consider **ALL things of that type** NOT just the Architecture of a piece. For example, when considering the Architecture of an Application, we must consider that in terms of, and in the context of, the Architecture of all Applications. In this sense, there is no such thing as Architecture for Application 1, and Architecture for Application 2, and Architecture for Application n. There is only Application Architecture - the whole point of which is - that it is used across ALL applications, or at least Applications of a certain class, and that the number of classes is a much smaller number than the number of Applications. This applies regardless of the type of architecture we are considering (Business, Enterprise/Transformation, Solution, Application, Data, Infrastructure, etc).

This is in contrast, to Engineering, where the whole tends not to be engineered at the same time. For this reason, we say that we Engineer vertically, that is, we utilise horizontal Architectural Structures but build in an end to end fashion.

In direct conflict to Architecture, Engineering MUST consider performing engineering **ONLY for that piece**, and NOT Engineering of all other things of that type. Why, because engineering work, is only concerned with engineering the piece in question. It has no remit or budget or mandate to perform engineering on anything else. Of course, that does not mean engineering cannot use patterns and lessons learned form performing Engineering in the past, but this use of patterns is not the same as the creation and maintenance of patterns we perform in Architecture work.

Thus…

We Architect horizontally, systemically.

We Engineer vertically, specifically.

KEYPOINT:

Think (and Plan) Strategically (Architecture), Act Tactically (Engineering)..

ADOPTION:

C-Suite: Mandate that people Architect horizontally and Engineer vertically.

Questions to Ponder

- Do the Management in your Enterprise, know the difference between Architecture and Engineering?
- Do the Workers in your Enterprise, know the difference between Architecture and Engineering?
- Does your Enterprise use Architecture and Engineering appropriately?
- If not, what problems are created?

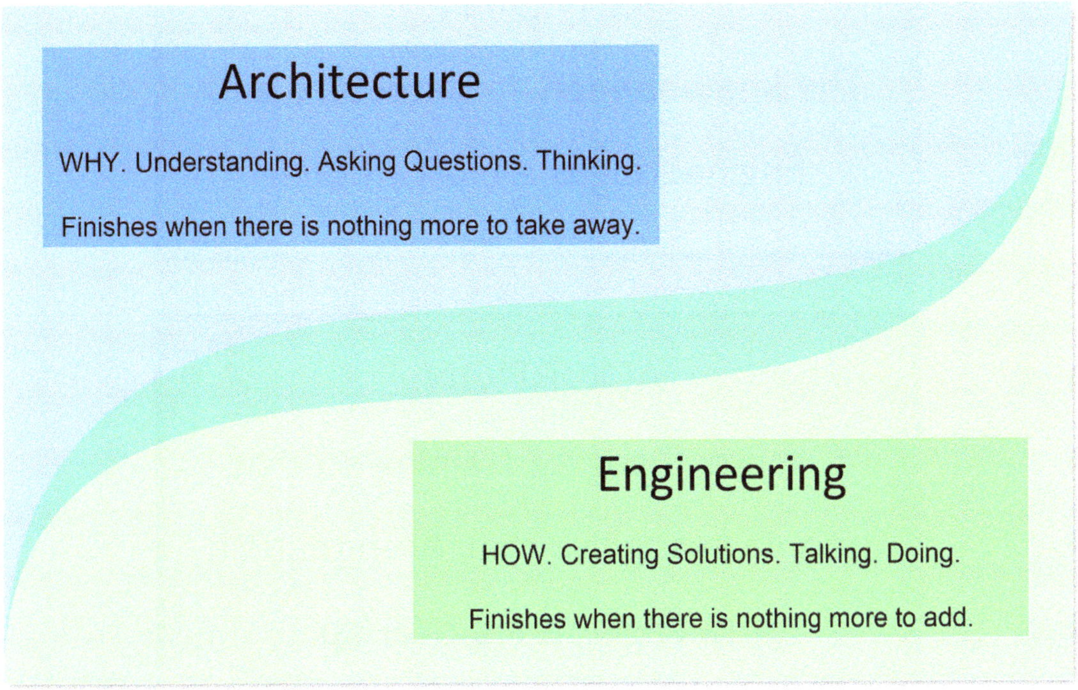

In practice, there is of course an overlap between Architecture and Engineering. The overlap may be small or may be large depending on the problem in hand. This tends to decide whether one person is required to perform both roles or if two people who specialise in each are required.

In this day and age, thinking about things seems to be viewed as a very bad thing as no discernible progress is being made. It should be noted that all the major advancements since time began have come from people thinking about things rather than doing - at least initially. This is not to say that everyone should sit around thinking about things and not doing anything. Doing things informs thinking and thinking informs doing. This is the yin and yang where balance must be achieved for best results and progress. No one ever suggested that people should stop doing things, but it is common for people to suggest that people should stop thinking about things "Just do it!" - not explicitly because when you say it explicitly, as I have just done, it sounds ludicrous in the extreme, but in practice, in life, in the day to day run of things, thinking is routinely put on the back burner as the next urgent (but probably unimportant) thing becomes the focus.

One of the differences between doing and thinking is that doing things has many limitations. Thinking has no literally no limitations. It is hardly surprising therefore that innovation and progress comes more from thinking than doing, albeit you do not see the fruits until something is built. For example, the fantastic smartphones we have today did not come from doing things, they can from thinking about what could be done. Thinking created the catalyst and doing made it happen. They had to be envisaged first. In that way, engineering places limitations on architecting however, architecting pushes those limitations and boundaries and thereby advances Engineering.

KEYPOINT:

The line between Architecture and Engineering is a blurred one.

ADOPTION:

C-Suite: Instigate training so that people recognise that Architecture and Engineering overlap.

Questions to Ponder

- Do you agree that Architecture is more about Why, while engineering is more about How?
- What do other people in your Enterprise believe?
- If there is not a common understanding, does this create problems?
- If so, what is the impact of those problems?

Culture > Architecture & Engineering > Overlap > Inter Phase

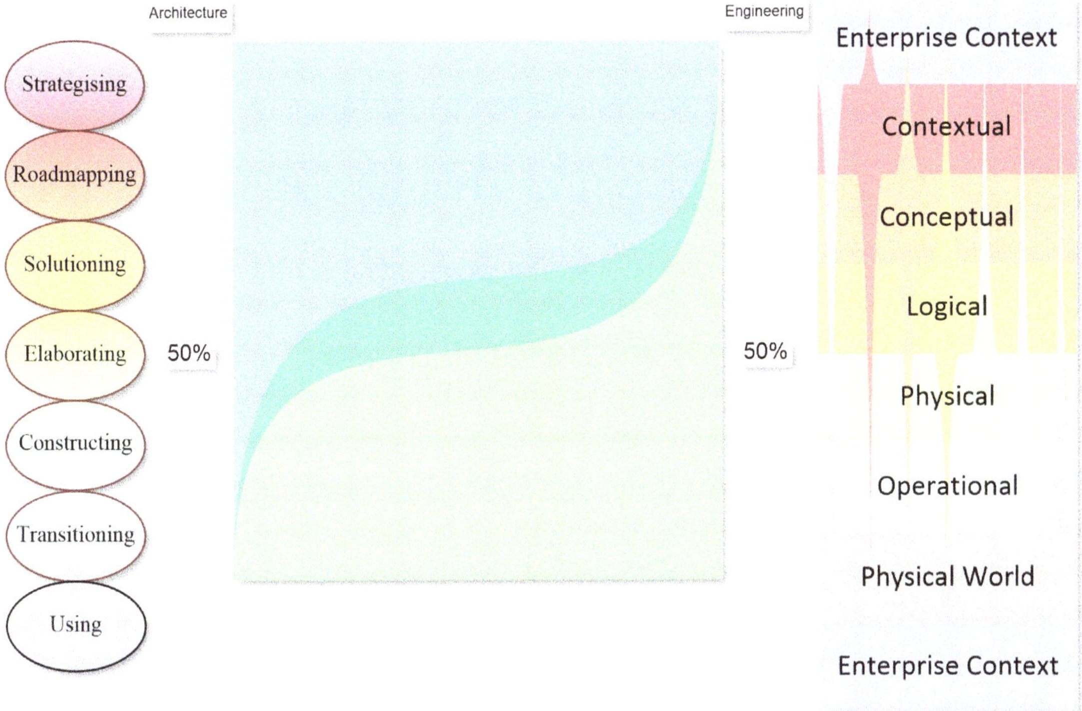

From the perspective of the entire Transformation domain, Architecture is performed more at the top of the stack and less at the bottom. Conversely Engineering is performed more at the bottom of the stack and less at the top.

The further down the stack we go the more concrete things become, and the further up the stack we go, the more abstract things become. This does not mean we are saying that there is no Engineering happening at the top and there is no Architecture happening at the bottom.

KEYPOINT:

Architecture is performed largely in the early phases of Transformation, while Engineering is performed largely in the later phases.

ADOPTION:

C-Suite: Instigate training so that people recognise that Architecture is performed largely in the early phases of Transformation, while Engineering is performed largely in the later phases.

Questions to Ponder

- Does your Enterprise recognise that people working towards the top of the Transformation stack are more Architects than Engineers?
- Does your Enterprise recognise that people working towards the bottom of the Transformation stack are more Engineers than Architects?
- If not, does this create any problems?
- Does this create any opportunities for education?

Culture > Architecture & Engineering > Overlap > Intra Phase

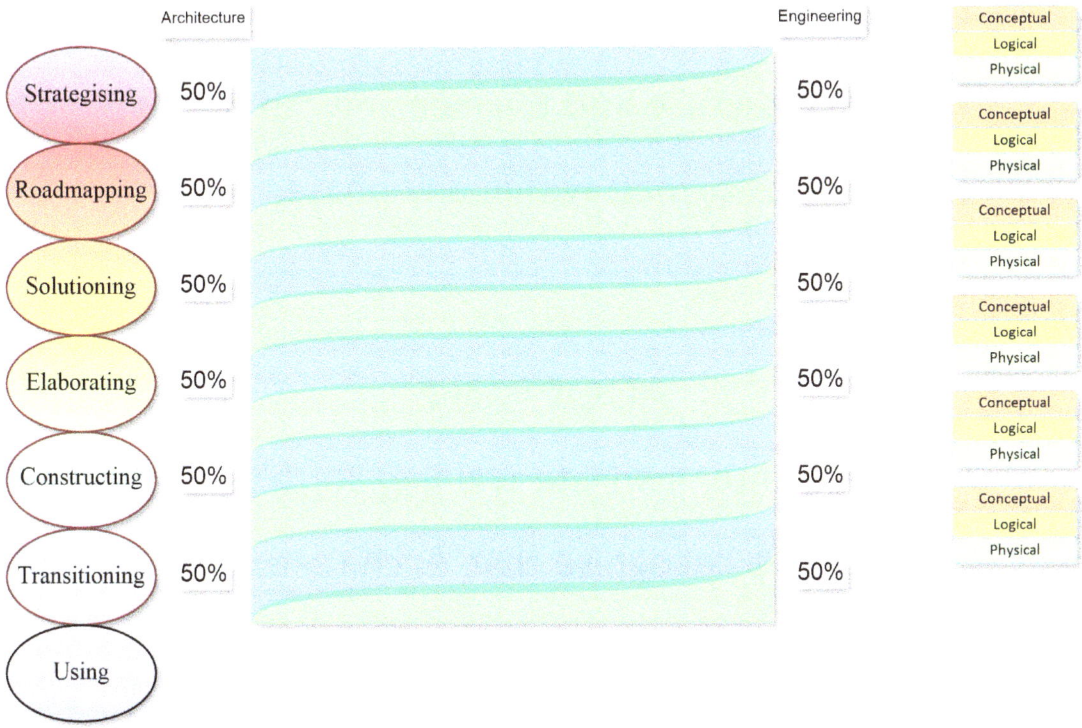

Architecture and Engineering map on to the fundamental phases of Transformation, and within each phase (depending on the Complexity of the information being worked upon).

Consequently the reality is a (potentially confusing) mixture of Architecture and Engineering which probably goes a long way to explain why there is such confusion and debate about how they are related and where they fit into the Transformation cascade. The truth is, they fit everywhere!

KEYPOINT:

Architecture and Engineering can be performed within any phase.

ADOPTION:

C-Suite: Instigate training so that people recognise that Architecture and Engineering are skills that can be applied anywhere.

Questions to Ponder

- Considering each phase of Transformation, do people who work there think of themselves primarily as Architects or Engineers or a mixture?
- Which phase of Transformation do you primarily work in?
- Do you consider yourself to be primarily an Architect or Engineer or a mixture?

Culture > Architecture & Engineering > Overlap > Overall

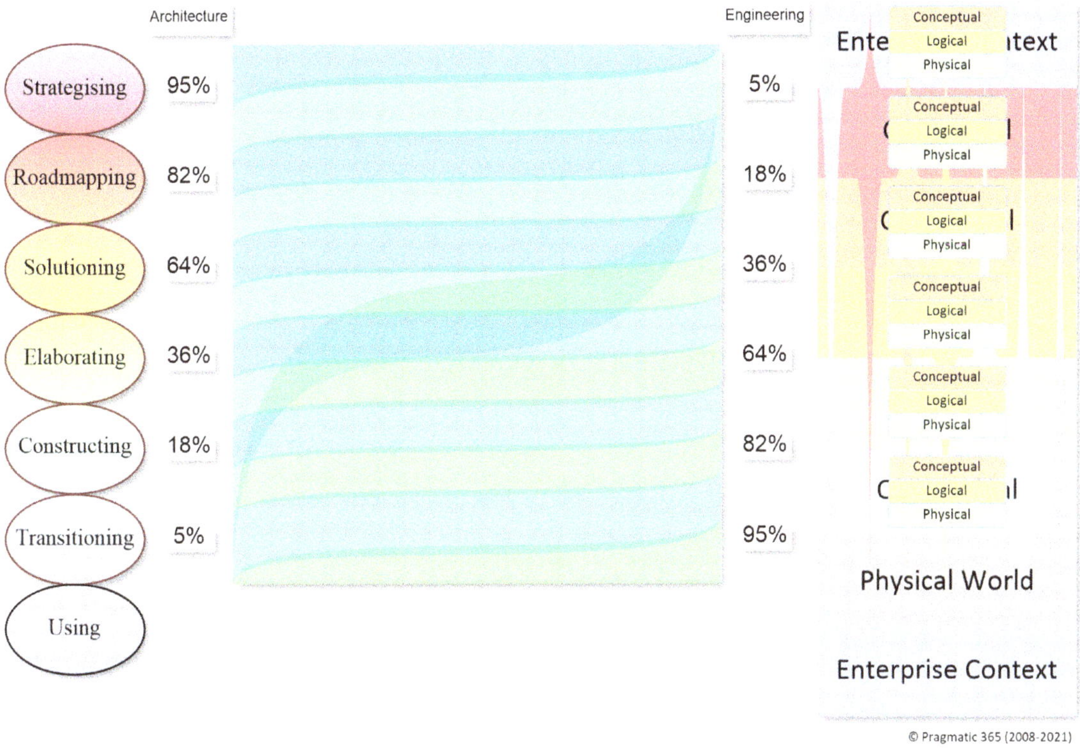

In many ways, the key to Transformation happening in a coherent, holistic fashion is the Architecture and Engineering Disciplines working together in harmony.

It is natural that the drive is always towards Engineering because it is Engineering that actually produces the tangible things that people want, but this overwhelming desire must be tempered and balanced by Architecture where appropriate. And while it is true that Architecture without Engineering is pointless, it is also true to say that Engineering without Architecture is foolhardy at best and at worst downright dangerous. And this risk increases as complexity and volatility rises.

The yin and yang of Architecture and Engineering is built upon the concept of the Thinking Mind-set and the Doing Mind-set. Research by psychologists Arie Kruglanski, Tory Higgins, and their colleagues suggests that we have two complementary motivational systems: the "thinking" system and the "doing" system - and we're generally only capable of using one at a time.

Think about how you best generate new ideas. Often, you "brainstorm" or try to come up with as many ideas as possible. That is called diverging and requires our thinking system. At other times, you need to evaluate those ideas and figure out which ones are best. That is called converging, and it requires the activation of the doing system.

KEYPOINT:

The relationship between Architecture and Engineering as we move from the top to the bottom phases is complex.

ADOPTION:

C-Suite: Instigate training so that people recognise that the application of Architecture and Engineering can be useful in any phase.

Questions to Ponder

- Are the Architecture and Engineering disciplines recognised in your Enterprise?
- Are they working in harmony or not?
- If not, what will you do to increase the harmony?

Architect	Engineer	Consultant
A person who knows very little, about a great deal, and keeps knowing less and less about more and more, until he knows practically nothing about everything.	A person who knows a great deal about very little, and keeps knowing more and more about less and less, until he knows practically everything about nothing.	A person that starts out knowing practically everything about everything, but ends up knowing nothing about anything, due to his association with architects and engineers.

- Aglaia Daae

{{Abdul Aziz}}

This is a little joke, but like all jokes, there is usually some grain of truth in it. In this case, there's a whole bag of rice and contains an important message!

Architects are generalists who look at the big picture. Since no one has the bandwidth to know everything about everything, an obvious side effect is that the more things they know about, the less bandwidth they have to drill into the details of those things.

Engineers are of course, the opposite, being specialists, who look are the small detailed picture. Since no one has the band width to know everything about everything, an obvious side effect is that the more detail they know about some thing, the less bandwidth they have to look at the bigger picture.

This intensely important distinction is imperative for the management of Enterprises to understand, not only from the point of view of needing both, but from the point of view of making people happy in the roles they perform and the effectiveness and efficiency by which they perform them.

Putting someone with an Architects brain in an Engineering job, or someone with an Engineers brain in an Architecture job, will make both feel hopelessly lost and depressed, which is guaranteed to make their work ineffective and inefficient. The Enterprise loses, the employee loses.

KEYPOINT:

Know and exploit the fundamental difference between Architects and Engineers.

ADOPTION:

Management: Ensure that Architects are give Architects jobs and Engineers are given Engineering.

Questions to Ponder

- Are you more of an Engineer or an Architect or are you both?
- Who in your Enterprise is an Engineer in an Architect's role?
- Are they happy?
- Who in your Enterprise is an Architect in an Engineer's role?
- Are they happy?
- How can your Enterprise exploit the differences between Architects and Engineers?

Architecture tends to be more about...		Engineering tends to be more about...
Art	*About*	Science
Why	*Looking*	How
The Problem	*Undertanding*	The Solution
Outside-In	*Think in terms of*	Inside-Out
Whole	*Focus*	Parts
Why > What	*Translation*	What > How
Uncertainty	*Deal in*	Certainty
Opportunity	*Impossible is a*	Constraint
Abstraction	*Function*	Elaboration
Nothing more to Remove	*Finished when*	Nothing more to Add
Eraser / Mind	*Important Tool*	Pencil / Hands
Thinking	*Work*	Doing
What is yet to come	*Consider*	What has been
Engineer	*Best Friend*	Architect
Client	*Driven by*	Architect
Breadth, Big Picture	*View*	Depth, Big Detail
Paints Them	*Pictures*	Takes Them
Long Term	*Wins*	Short Term
Impossible	*Cost Justification*	Possible
Intangible	*True Value*	Tangible
Love it	*When they are wrong*	Hate it
Creativity	*Change*	Innovation
Lines	*Focus*	Boxes
Immortal / Permanent	*Sustainability*	Mortal / Temporary

It is not easy (Impossible? – But that's why I like it!) to just state what Architecture and Engineering are. The relationship between these two disciplines is complex and more grey than black and white. And so, the best way to more fully understand them is to compare and contrast them in various dimensions.

Architecture tends to be more **art** than science.

Engineering tends to be more **science**, than art.

Architecture is more about looking up (**Why**) than looking down (**How**).

Engineering is more about looking down (**How**) than looking up (**Why**).

Architecture is more about understanding the **Problem**.

Engineering is more about understanding the **Solution**.

Architects tend to think in terms of **outside-in**.

Engineers tend to think in terms of **inside-out**.

Architects are aware of the parts of a system, but tend to **focus on the whole.**

Engineers are aware of the whole system, but tend to **focus on the parts**.

Architects tend to be more concerned with the **why > what** translation with a little of the **how**.

Engineers tend to be more concerned with the **what > how to** translation with a little of the **why**.

Architects tend to deal in **uncertainty**.

Engineers tend to deal in **certainty**.

Architects tend to see **impossible** as an **opportunity**.

Engineers tend to see **impossible** as a **constraint**.

Architecture is more about **omission**, **composition**, **generalisation** and **idealisation**, than it is about inclusion, decomposition, specialisation or realisation.

Engineering is more about **inclusion**, **decomposition**, **specialisation** and **realisation**, than it is about omission, composition, generalisation or idealisation.

An Architect knows their job is done when there is **nothing more to take away**.

An Engineer knows their job is done when there is **nothing more to add**.

The most important tool for an Architect is their **eraser**.

The most important tool for an Engineer is their **pencil**.

Architects tend to **think**.

Engineers tend to **do**.

Architects tend to consider things from the perspective of **what is yet to come**.

Engineers tend to consider things from the perspective of **what has been**.

An Architect doesn't get **what** they want until an Engineer Builds it.

An Engineer doesn't know **what** to Build until an Architect specifies it.

An Architect doesn't know **why** to Architect something until a Client specifies it.

An Engineer doesn't know **why** to build something until an Architect tells specifies it.

To "do" Architecture you need **breadth**, to see the **big picture**.

To "do" Engineering you need **depth**, to see the **big detail**.

Architects **paint pictures**. An interpretation of reality.

Engineers **take pictures**. A record of reality.

You Architect **long term wins**.

You Engineer **quick wins**.

You **cannot** cost justify Architecture.

You **can** cost justify Engineering.

The true value of Architecture is **intangible**.

The true value of Engineering is **tangible**.

Architects tend to **like** to find out when they are wrong.

Engineers tend to **hate** to find out when they were wrong.

Architects tend to be more about unleashing the potential of the mind to conceive new ideas (**Creativity**).

Engineers tend to be more about introducing change into relatively stable systems (**Innovation**)

Architecture is more about the lines (**Relationships**) than the boxes

Engineering is more about the boxes (**Objects**) that the lines.

Architecture tends to be immortal and permanent.

Engineering tends to be mortal and temporary.

KEYPOINT:

Architecture and Engineering, bring important things to the table, and makes the whole much more than the sum of its parts.

ADOPTION:

C-Suite: Instigate training so that people recognise the differences between Architecture and Engineering, and use both appropriately.

Questions to Ponder

- Are you more of an Engineer or an Architect or are you both?
- How much time are you allowed to spend "thinking" rather than "doing"?
- If you were given the space to think more, would you be better at your job?
- How many Architects does it take to change a light bulb?
- (None - It's an Engineering problem ;-)
- Does your Enterprise use Architects and Engineers in an appropriate way?
- Can you think of other ways that Architects and Engineers contrast each other?

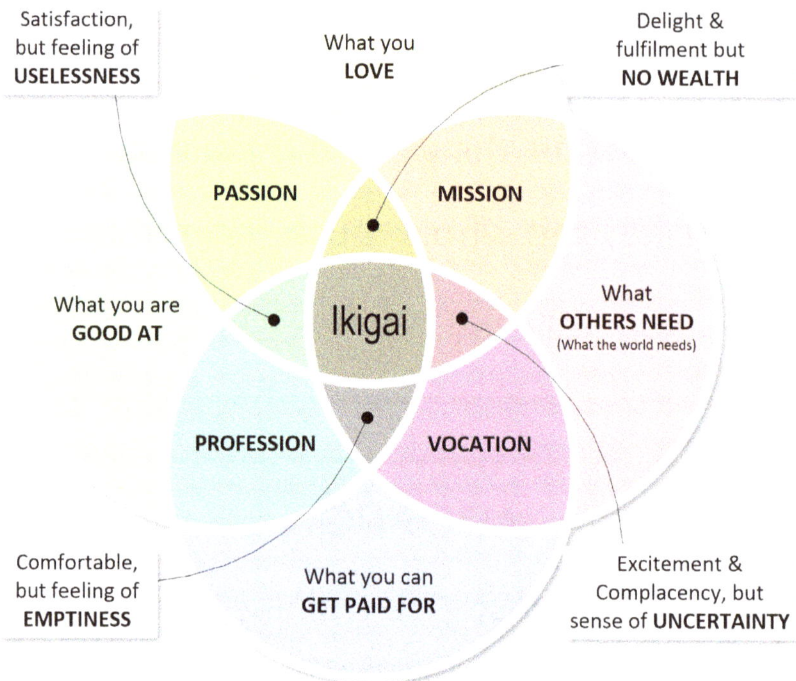

Are you an Architect in an Engineers job? A manager in an Architects job? An Engineer in an Architects job. An Engineer in a Managers job?

While others may decide or confer titles on you, we suggest you look into yourself, your soul, and decide first and foremost who the real you is, and then make any changes necessary, so that the real you shines through.

Here we discuss a diagram from a book called "The Japanese Secret to a Long and Happy Life" by Francesc Miralles and Hector Garcia. Like most models, it is a powerful aid to thinking about yourself (and others) and can help you decide if you are in the right job, or if you are doing the right things for the right reasons.

It considers that there are 4 main areas:

- What you **LOVE** - This equates to what you like to do. What gets you out of bed in the morning. What you would choose to do if there were no other restrictions.
- What you are **GOOD AT** - This equates to what you are good at. There will be some things you are good at, and like doing, There will be other things you are good at, that you do not like doing.
- What **OTHERS NEED** - This was originally titled "What the world needs" but the word "world" puts a domain constraint on the question that need not be there. To one person "the world" may literally be the world. To others "the world" may mean their family, or the company they work for. As we have learned before "Context is King"™ and therefore you need to place the context you wish on the model to be able to answer its questions.
- What you can **GET PAID FOR** – This equates to getting something of value that you can exchange for other things you need, aka money.

Since you are in control of the context, it allows you to utilise the model in different contexts. For example, one to represent your home life where "the world" is your family and "what you can get paid for" is the respect of your family (and the "payment" of your family achieving their Ikigai) and another to represent your working life where the company you work for is "the world" and the "payment" is your salary.

Where these primary domains overlap is where happiness (and sadness) lies.

At the intersection of what you are good at, and what you need lies your **PROFESSION**.

At the intersection of what you are good at, and what you love, lies your **PASSION**.

At the intersection of what others need, and what you need lies your **VOCATION**.

And, at the intersection of what others need, and what you love, lies your **MISSION**.

The other intersections illustrate areas of partial Ikigai where three of the four aspects are fulfilled but one is not.

- Satisfying what you love, what you are good at, and what you need, leaves a feeling of **USELESSNESS**, because you are not doing what **OTHERS NEED**.
- Satisfying what others need, what you love, and what you are good at, means you have **NO WEALTH**, because you are not doing what you can **GET PAID FOR**.
- Satisfying what you need, what others need, and what you love, leaves you with a sense of **UNCERTAINTY**, because you are not doing what you are **GOOD AT**.
- And, satisfying what you are good at, what you need, and what others need, leaves you with a feeling of **EMPTINESS**, because you are not doing what you **LOVE**.

Ikigai, is that perfect balance where you balance what you need, with what others need, with what you are good at, with what you love.

It would be nice if people can truly achieve Ikigai, but for the most part, many of us do not. From my professional life context (at this point in time – because things always change) I would say that I exist in the "Delight & fulfilment but no WEALTH. That is:

- I am doing what I truly love to do (maturing the Transformation domain of Enterprises).
- I (believe) I am good at it.
- I (believe) I am supplying what others need – others being Enterprises all over the world (even though they may not realise they need it)

So, I feel delight and fulfilment, but have no wealth. For me this is fine, because I place a much higher value on doing things I enjoy, that I am good at, and that help others, than any monetary gain. Money is not what gets me out of bed in the morning. The other three together do.

KEYPOINT:

A happy productive person, balances what they are good at, with what they love, what others need, and what they want.

ADOPTION:

C-Suite: Initiate a review to allow people to balance what they are good at, with what they love, what others needs are, and what their needs are.

Questions to Ponder

- What do you love and what are you good at? Are they the same things?
- If not, what are you going to do about that?
- What can you get paid for and what do others needs that you can provide? Are they the same things?
- If not, what are you going to do about that?
- How does your home life Ikigai map, compare to your professional life Ikigai map?
- If you were only able to satisfy 3 out of the 4 primary areas, which ones would you chose and why?

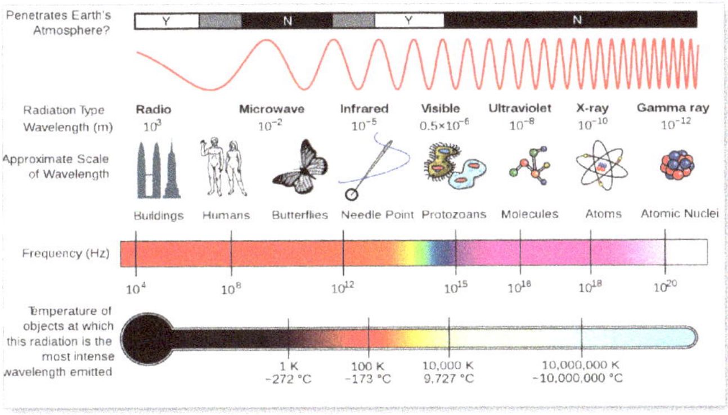

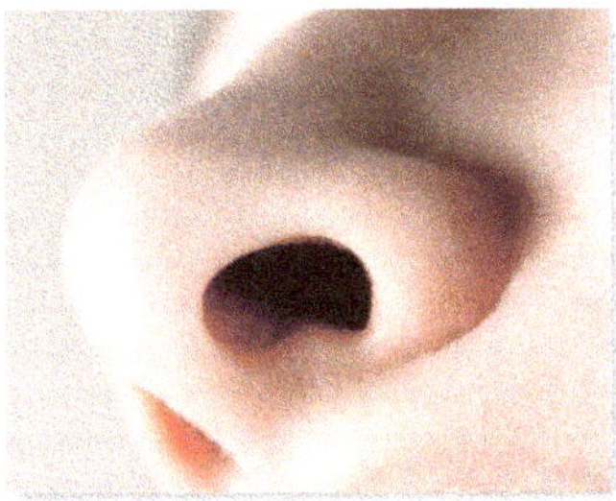

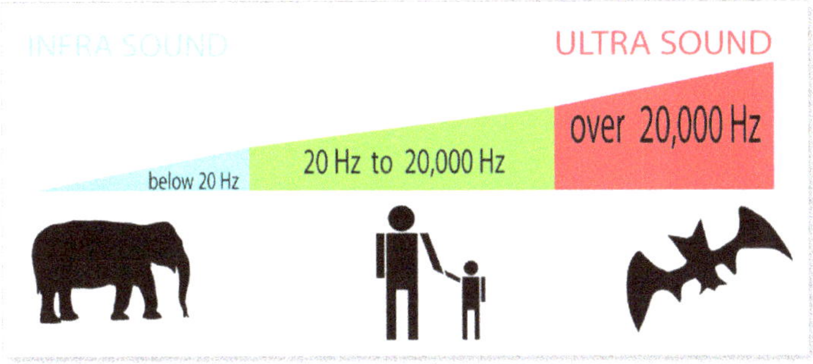

One of the curses ("my name is Legion, for we are many") of being an Architect is that they often can see things, as plain as day, that others who are not Architects cannot see. This does NOT mean that Architects are in some way superior or more important. It just means they are different. It's like everyone else can only see visible light, but Architects can see the full spectrum from infrared to ultraviolet and beyond. Architects can hear what others cannot hear, feel what others cannot feel, smell what others cannot smell and taste what others cannot taste.

But there is another curse far worse than all of these. And that is that Architects can see into the future. I don't mean, of course, that they can tell you the winner of the 4:15 as Ascot! What I mean is that they have the uncanny ability (some may call it a sixth sense) to be able to foresee things, to think ahead. In fact it's more than a sense, it is almost what defines them to be Architects in the first place. Ignore an Architect because he is talking about things in the future and there is no point in employing him in the first place!

Actually, although everyone knows and is taught that there are five senses, this is in fact wrong (as are many things taught in school!). The five senses we commonly know about come from Aristotle who also got it wrong when he said that there are only four elements (Earth, Fire, Water, and Air). Today, it is thought that there are actually anywhere from nine to twenty one senses, for example; Pressure, Itch, Thermoception, Proprioception, Tension Sensors, Nociception, Equilibrioception, Stretch Receptors, Chemoreceptors, Thirst, Hunger, Magnetoception and Time.

Architects do not necessarily discover new things, more they discover new ways of seeing existing things. Putting things "in a new light".

"New Light through Old Windows"

- Chris Rea

Architects expose things that can provide new insights into existing things. When people see **New Light through Old Windows** it can change fundamentally how they see and approach things, the decisions they take and why. This is one thing that POET helps to do, but it's a difficult thing to see - hence the references to SEPs and the Magic Eye picture at the beginning.

Since Architects can see, hear, taste, feel, and smell things that others cannot and also have the ability to peer into the future, they therefore know things that others do not know. Some may say, secrets. And as someone once said:

> "The secret of business is to know something that nobody else knows".
>
> ***- Aristotle Onassis.***

It may be surprising to people, that the leaders of Enterprises do not see the value that Architects can bring to all domains rather than just IT. In time they will. I know because I am an Architect and I can see into the future ;-)

KEYPOINT:

"The secret of business is to know something that nobody else knows."

- Aristotle Onassis

ADOPTION:

C-Suite: Mandate that people should exploit the fact Architects should be exploited to easily see things that others find difficult or impossible to see.

Questions to Ponder

- Would you like to see things others cannot?
- Would you like know things others do not?
- Do you think seeing into the future is valuable?
- We are very happy to use animals that have super-senses like the dogs to sniff out drugs and explosives, so why do people shy away from using that strange "animal" called an Architect?
- Does your Enterprise shy away from Architects?

"Impossible is just a big word thrown around by small men who find it easier to live in the world they've been given than to explore the power they have to change it. **Impossible is not a fact. It's an opinion.** Impossible is not a declaration. It's a dare. Impossible is potential. Impossible is temporary. Impossible is nothing."

- Muhammad Ali

"It always seems impossible until its done."

- Nelson Mandela

"To believe a thing impossible is to make it so."

- French Proverb

"Everything is theoretically impossible, until it is done."

- Robert A. Heinlein

"We would accomplish many more things if we did not think of them as impossible."

- Vince Lombardi

"Never tell a young person that anything cannot be done. God may have been waiting centuries for someone ignorant enough of the impossible to do that very thing."

- G. M. Trevelyan

"Every noble work is at first impossible."

- Thomas Carlyle

"So many of our dreams at first seem impossible, then they seem improbable, and then, when we summon the will, they soon become inevitable."

- Christopher Reeve

Impossible is why Architects get out of bed in the morning. But even though they strive to achieve "impossible" things, their job is, in itself also "impossible".

Being an Architect could be looked on more as an affliction - a cross to bear. Architects can't stop being Architects (which tends to really irritate people who are not Architects!). Being an Architect is a state of mind, a way of being. For an Architect 1+1 often equals 3, or more likely 1+1 equals blue! Architects tend to break the rules. For when you break the rules, you change the game.

Architects know and accept that there are things that they do not know about and go looking for them (remember Donald Rumsfeld?). Most of these things do not magically appear to them, they appear to them because they go looking for them. They wheedle them out from all the background noise. While most people bask in their knowledge and experience, an architect knows there are things he does not know about and actively goes about trying to find them. An architect is much more interested in what he doesn't know that what he knows. He is often surprised by what he finds, but never bored.

Because an Architect tends to see things (and find things) others cannot, they tend always to be in a position of exposing things that were not known, and therefore not taken account of, when decisions were made. This puts them in a position of seemingly to always be challenging decisions and wanting those decisions changed or in some cases reversed. This is not something that is generally welcomed, especially by the type of people who are responsible for making those decisions.

Humans are good at spotting patterns - our brains are hardwired for visual pattern recognition. However Architects are different for two reasons. Firstly, because they are more adept at seeing patterns in concepts and thoughts, and secondly, because they can see patterns based on sparse or very limited volumes of information. If the volume of information is large (like a hi resolution photo) anyone can spot the pattern, but if the volume of information is low (like a pixelated photo) only an architect can "squint" with his brain and still see things of value.

It's not so much about people not understanding what an Architect is saying, but more about people finding it difficult to see the thing the Architect is talking about in the first place. Most people do not (are not allowed to) spend the time to do so.

An Architect is an investigator (like Judge Judy!) and one of the tools of an investigator is cynicism - he doesn't believe anything until he can prove it or at least not have any feeling that he is not getting the whole truth. The yardstick of that is understanding. When an Architect gets an answer to a question and the answer doesn't make sense (a big part of that is common sense) he asks more questions. This irritates people who are hiding things or do not know what they are talking about and then begin to call the Architect "confrontational" or "rude" or "inappropriate" or any other of a number of vague negative words. When that happens, an Architect knows he is onto something.

Many many people go through life unchallenged. Talking about things that they do not really understand - possibly just repeating what they heard someone else say, saying things that while not bare-faced lies, could be considered to be economical with the truth. Many more people go through life also hearing things that perhaps they think are wrong or do not make sense but they do not say anything. They do not question and they do not challenge. The reason for this is not because they are bad people, but is rooted in psychology and man's deep desire to "not upset the applecart" and to be friends and get on with everyone. Architects do not think or work like that. In a way, they could be thought of being socially inept which can easily come across as being rude, confrontational, arrogant or disrespectful. This is not because they are bad people that should be controlled or ignored. The more you try to control or ignore an Architect, the more vocal he is likely to become. Paying them lip-service or trying to placate them is like adding fuel to a fire and is usually a recipe for disaster.

Another problem with Architects is that they tend to be in a minority. Perhaps less than 1% of all people are intrinsically an Architect. Add to this the fact that they tend to see things that others cannot see, and it tends to mean they are also in a minority in terms of their views and ideas and there is great scope for the majority to ignore them as it is usually thought that the majority must always right - "You are the only one that thinks that" - aka you must be wrong because the majority must be right.

Another problem with being an Architect (and making a difference) is that we, by definition, **only see and only raise fundamental problems**. By definition this either means a big grand plan needs to be changed or if the work has been going on that a lot of work has to potentially be thrown away. Both of these things can (and usually do) create massive political problems as the onus is usually on someone "important" having to either change something big he/she previously announced or admit they already wasted a whole lot of money, time and resources. That's why Management should involve Architects in matters as early as possible. It's almost a case of - "if you don't involve us early enough, you better not involve us at all because you probably won't like what we are going to say!"

Architects can often be accused of living in a "perfect world". This is really just a perception problem. Because they can see things clearly that others cannot see, or cannot easily see, or do not want to see, they can see those things are achievable while others think they are not.

In general, people see disagreements as confrontations - and people in general really hate confrontations and tend to do anything and everything to avoid them. That, of course, does not mean that they do not tell anyone, it just means they tell the "wrong" people. How many times have you received bad service in a restaurant or from a call centre but didn't say anything at the time, but then complained to your friends about it later? There is a saying in retail - a happy customer will tell one friend, an unhappy one will tell ten.

"A wise man gets more use from his enemies than a fool from his friends."

- Baltasar Gracian

Of course, with the advent of the internet, social media and YouTube, if you are unlucky, one unhappy customer will tell thirteen million people - as happened with the famous "United Breaks Guitars" case. United Airlines concentrated on saving $1,200. Their stock price fell 10% four days after the YouTube video was posted wiping $180 million off the company's value. The resulting bad publicity cost them unimaginably more.

But we digress. The bigger the disagreement, the greater the perceived confrontation. There is also an element that the person who believes they hold the most "power" tends to see the other person as confrontational rather than the other way round. If the disagreement is about something small or of no real significance the confrontation is very small, but if the disagreement is about something of fundamental importance then confrontation can be huge. Bearing in mind that Architects **only** talk about things of fundamental significance, it could be said that appearing to be confrontational is not only possible, it is mandatory!

> "As an Architect, if you aren't annoying someone, you aren't doing your job properly"

- Pragmatic

The new light Architects expose (through the old windows of peoples existing perceptions) is very challenging for many people as this basically takes them out of their comfort zone. Big time. Most people do not like that at all. Most people are happy to continue to live their lives, in their familiar comfortable pond, and they react in all manner of negative ways when someone tries to explain there is life outside their pond, especially when it impacts their pond in a big or fundamental way. They are not bad people.

So, where do architects "fit"? The simple answer is, nowhere and everywhere. They don't really fit anywhere! This is why many architects always have an uneasy feeling of being different and misunderstood.

> "When green is all there is to be
> It could make you wonder why, but why wonder?
> Why Wonder, I am green and it'll do fine, it's beautiful!
> And I think it's what I want to be."

- Kermit the Frog

It 'ain't easy, being green.

http://youtu.be/hpilWMWWVco

KEYPOINT:

"Every noble work is at first, impossible."

- Thomas Carlyle

ADOPTION:

C-Suite: When asking an Architect a question, do not expect an Engineering answer.

Questions to Ponder

- How do you react when an Architect talks about unknown unknowns?
- How do you react when you cannot see what an Architect is trying to explain?
- How do you react when an Architect is in the minority?
- How do you react when an Architect exposes (fundamental) things that may cause you to change a previous decision or cause you to "throw away" work?

"Our job is to give the client … not what he wants, but what he never dreamed that he wanted; and when he gets it, he recognizes it as something he wanted all the time."

- Sir Denys Lasdon

Some notable quotes that I believe illustrates what an Architect does,

> "Architecture at all levels provides the Landing strip of intent for any viable implementation to touch down on."
>
> - {{Gareth Llewellyn}}

> "An Architect knows his job is done, not when there is nothing more to add, but when there is nothing more to take away."
>
> ***- Based on a quote from Antoine de Saint-Exupéry, Airman's Odyssey***

> "The architect must be a prophet… a prophet in the true sense of the term… if he can't see at least ten years ahead don't call him an architect."
>
> ***- Frank Lloyd Wright***

> "The most important tool for an Architect is his eraser."
>
> ***- Frank Lloyd Wright***

> "Every great architect is - necessarily - a great poet. He must be a great original interpreter of his time, his day, his age."
>
> ***- Frank Lloyd Wright***

> "There is nothing more uncommon than common sense."
>
> ***- Frank Lloyd Wright***

> "All fine architectural values are human values, else not valuable."

- Frank Lloyd Wright

"Early in life, I had to choose between honest arrogance and hypocritical humility. I chose honest arrogance and have seen no occasion to change."

- Frank Lloyd Wright

"Form follows function- that has been misunderstood. Form and function should be one, joined in a spiritual union."

- Frank Lloyd Wright

"A great architect is not made by way of a brain nearly so much as he is made by way of a cultivated, enriched heart. "

- Frank Lloyd Wright

"Our job is to give the client … not what he wants but what he never dreamed that he wanted; and when he gets it, he recognizes it as something he wanted all the time."

- Sir Denys Lasdon

"A good Architect can't sleep because a piece of the puzzle is missing. A bad Architect can't sleep because his conscience won't let him."

- Unknown

KEYPOINT:

"Architecture provides the Landing strip of intent, for any viable implementation to land on."

- {{Gareth Llewellyn}}

ADOPTION:

C-Suite: If you know what you want, but don't know what you need, ask an Architect.

Questions to Ponder

- Do you agree with Sir Denys Lasdon?
- If not, how would you describe the job of an Architect (of any domain)?
- What do others in your Enterprise believe?

How can you tell the difference between an Architect and a Charlatan?

**DO NOT TURN THE PAGE.
YET….**

Please take some time to consider an answer to this question.

Think about the kinds of things an Architect and a Charlatan might say.

Think about how you would determine (from how they speak and what they say) which one was an Architect and which one was a Charlatan?

Then, turn the page to find the shocking answer….

You can't!

Both talk of future benefit that is impossible or difficult to quantify and understand.

- The Architect speaks in this way because it's true.
- The Charlatan speaks in this way to draw you in.

Both say that they will have fantastic effects.

- The Architect speaks in this way because it's true.
- The Charlatan speaks in this way to draw you in.

Both say they can see into the future.

- The Architect speaks in this way because it's true.
- The Charlatan speaks in this way to draw you in.

Of course, from the perspective of what they do, they are very different, but from the perspective of someone who doesn't know if you are a Charlatan or not, they are almost indistinguishable by the things they say. It all sounds a bit like "smoke and mirrors".

So, as an Architect, don't be surprised if people look at you as a potential Charlatan.

That is the way an Architect looks to many people - especially the kind of people Architects are "selling" to, such as Leaders, Executives, Managers, CxO's, Directors etc. These kinds of people have spent many many years listening to the claims and promises of hundreds of vendors who all want to sell them the next bottle of snake-oil and will promise anything just to make the sale.

Architects need to accept that inconvenient truth and deal with it.

Face it.

Talk about it.

Openly.

Because if you don't, many people will view you as a Charlatan, whether you like it or not, whether you realise it or not.

They are not bad people, they are just a product of the Context they operate in. A context that consists of a never ending supply of salesman and vendors telling them that their offering is the next big things that has will solve all their problems.

KEYPOINT:

"The value of Architecture is intangible.

If it were tangible, it would be Engineering."

- Kevin Lee Smith

ADOPTION:

C-Suite: When asking an Architect a question, do not expect a tangible answer.

Questions to Ponder

- Do you or your Enterprise view Architects as Charlatans, promising snake oil that will cure all ills?
- Do you or your Enterprise view Architects as people that talk in future promise that cannot really be objectively quantified?

Culture > The Architect > The Pragmatic Architect Creed

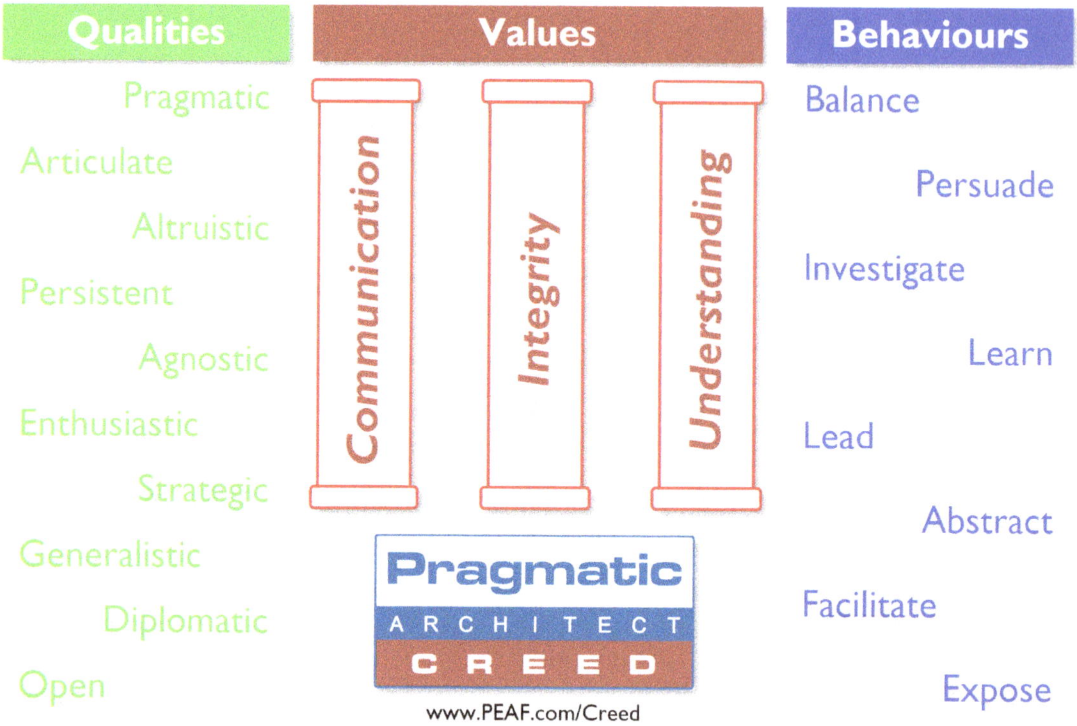

The **Pragmatic** Architect Creed (PAC) is a set of values, qualities and behaviours that an Architect in any domain should abide by. It effectively defines the culture of a **Pragmatic** Architect.

If a **Pragmatic** Architect is asked to do something which conflicts with the Creed, or is aware that another **Pragmatic** Architect is acting in conflict with the values, he or she should raise a concern within their own department. Their department should investigate their concern. If the **Pragmatic** Architect remains dissatisfied following the outcome of the investigation, they may bring a complaint to the **Pragmatic** Architect Commission. In some cases, the Commission may also hear a complaint direct.

You can sign the **Pragmatic** Creed at www.Pragmatic365.org/creed

Pillars

The creed defines of 3 main values:

- **Communication** – Recognising that open, honest and direct communication is key to both understanding and being understood.
- **Integrity** – Recognising that being a trusted advisor is key to being believed by our clients.
- **Understanding** – Recognising that understanding client's minds and getting clients to understand our mind is the backbone of what we do.

For each of these values, there are statements that a **Pragmatic** Architect should be able to recite, with their hand on their heart.

Communication

- I believe that communication is crucially important as an architect.
- I believe that communication is key to me understanding other people and getting others to understand me.
- I believe that without good communication, no relationship can survive or thrive.
- I evangelise the value of Architecture and its benefits.
- I strive to create a "safe environment" where people are free to express their views without fear of punishment or recrimination.
- I relate new things that people do not know to things that people already know.
- I can vehemently agree with someone about subject/point "A" when I have only recently vehemently disagreed with the same person about subject/point "B".
- I commit whatever time is required to explain and convince others when I am right.
- I can always explain the reasoning behind my views.
- I can clearly communicate contextual, conceptual, logical and complex issues and trade-offs to any audience.
- I am comfortable talking and presenting to large groups or individuals at any level.

Integrity

- I believe that integrity is crucially important as an architect.
- I believe that an architect's biggest asset is the trust he is afforded by the people he works for and the people he works with.
- I believe that without trust, no relationship can survive or thrive.
- I ensure the interests of the Enterprise as a whole are addressed even if they appear to conflict with immediate management.
- I stand up and give an unpalatable truth when no one else will, even though it may mean I lose my job.
- I will seek to terminate a consulting engagement early if it transpires that the customer can get no or little value by continuing.
- I always tell the truth.
- I never hide or disguise things.
- I tell clients what they need to hear, not what they want to hear.
- I welcome being proved wrong and if I am, admit it as soon as possible.
- I suggest only appropriate solutions - even if that is a 'pen and paper solution'.

Understanding

- I believe that understanding is crucially important as an architect.
- I believe that if we do not understand something, people cannot form opinions or solutions to problems.
- I believe that without understanding, no relationship can survive or thrive.
- I believe that the primary responsibility of an architect is to enable informed decision making.
- I believe that the most important question to ask is - Why?
- I see patterns and structure in everything from traffic congestion to Pop music and flowers.
- I spend more time understanding a problem domain than determining a solution.
- I spend more time asking questions and listening than I do talking.

- I can see disagreement between people when those people think they are in agreement and vice versa.
- I can abstract anything or idea to a logical and conceptual level.
- I constantly self-analyse what I do and how I do it to determine how to improve myself and my work.
- I know the difference between Architecture & Engineering.
- I know the difference between types of abstraction (Omission/Inclusion, Composition/Decomposition, Generalisation/Specialisation, Idealisation/Realisation) and when and how to use them effectively.
- I know the difference between types of Idealisation/Realisation (Contextual, Conceptual, Logical, Physical, Operational) and when and how to use them effectively.
- I know the difference between a model, a meta-model, and meta-meta-model.

Qualities

	Description	Rationale
Pragmatic	They are always looking to understand what the perfect solution can be but tempering that with a more commercial and tactical view that relates to the realities of getting things done.	Architects need to be able to see the long term perfect solution but they need to be able to temper that unattainable goal with the tactics of getting things done.
Articulate	They are at home communicating with everyone from the board to the graduate programmer or claims clerk and in scales from one to one to speaking to hundreds at conferences.	Communication is a major part of an Architects role. Being able to listen, ask the right questions, and explain things in words that people can understand from CEOs to the tea lady.
Altruistic	They are selfless, and always focused on what is best for the Enterprise not what is best for them.	Architects are 100% focused on the Enterprise they work for. Even if this means losing their own job.
Persistent	They will not be steamrollered and will stand up for what they believe in.	A good idea or a worthy point that needs to be made for the benefit of the Enterprise, needs to be made regardless of an environment that may not let that happen.
Agnostic	They see all things from Supercomputers to paper, pencils and people as possible solutions to business problems and will propose the most appropriate for any given context not what their favourite is.	Architecture is all about providing business value, not about and Architect's "favourite" things.
Enthusiastic	They are passionate and enthusiastic about what they do and how they do it.	Enthusiasm is an inspiring trait and Architects need to inspire others in order to affect and guide the culture of an Enterprise.
Strategic	They are focused on long term and lasting benefits rather than short term benefits which compromise long term objectives.	Long term and lasting benefits are more important strategically to an Enterprise.

Generalistic	They have a broad base of technical and business experience.	Architects deal with breadth rather than depth, and therefore need a broad range of business and technical skills.
Diplomatic	They are sensitive to other people's drivers and the political context.	Architecture is more to do with people and culture than anything else. Architects therefore need to be able to discuss often difficult and controversial subjects and truths with tact and sensitivity.
Open	They are open to critique, happy to be proved wrong, and will assimilate and apply new information as it arises.	Architects do not have all the answers. They need to be open to criticisms and open to adjusting their views as new information is exposed or the environment changes.

Behaviours

	Description	Rationale
Balance {{Tamás Nacsák}}	They balance a multitude of different and often competing factors in order to arrive at solutions that make the best of	The problems Architects solve are "wicked problems". Such problems do not have simple answers. Indeed, the questions they answer are also not simple.
Persuade	They persuade others of their views and the way forward rather than dictating.	Architects rely on others to achieve their aims and as such people must be persuaded of an approach. When people buy into an idea or approach they are much happier and much more productive.
Investigate	They have a nose to seek out things that don't make sense or could pose threats and risks, and the ability to get to the bottom of them.	Things that don't make sense are usually problems or opportunities. Either way, Architects need to be able to dig into things where necessary to expose them so that they can be addressed.
Learn	They pick up and assimilate new information quickly and easily and are always open to new ideas, businesses, technologies and processes.	Business and the world is an ever-changing place. New things are happening all the time and Architects need to quickly understand them and how they impact the business.
Lead	They lead, motivate, inspire and enable others to reach their potential and create the environment where people want to follow them.	Architecture is all about culture, and therefore to adopt and make the cultural changes required, Architects need to be able to take individuals and the Enterprise on a journey and that journey must be by mutual consent not by dictation.
Abstract	They abstract levels of detail to higher levels to aid understanding and to see hidden relationships and patterns.	Architecture is a lot about seeing structure and patterns. In order to do this an Architect needs to be able to see and synthesise these higher-level structures from underlying information that can be very detailed and/or incomplete.
Facilitate	They guide discussions and workshops in order to get the best out of people.	Architecture is a lot about communication and also about liberating information from others. It is also important to be able to guide discussions

		and to bring people together where there is agreement and to facilitate valued discussed where there are differences.
Expose	They seek to expose pertinent information to business leaders to enable them to make more informed decisions.	Decisions will get made regardless of whether full and/or pertinent facts are known. Architecture is all about making sure people who make decisions are fully aware of the risks, issues and implications before the decision is made.

KEYPOINT:

The Pragmatic Architects Creed™ sorts the wheat from the chaff.

ADOPTION:

C-Suite: Mandate the use of the Pragmatic Architects Creed™ to recruit Architects.

Questions to Ponder

- Would these Qualities and Behaviours be beneficial to your Enterprise?
- If so, in what parts of your Enterprise and in what roles?
- what happens to people who exhibit these Qualities and Behaviours in your Enterprise?
- Do you evaluate your current employees or new hires using these Qualities and Behaviours
- If not, which Qualities and Behaviours do you actively look for?
- Will you sign the Creed?

Culture > Language

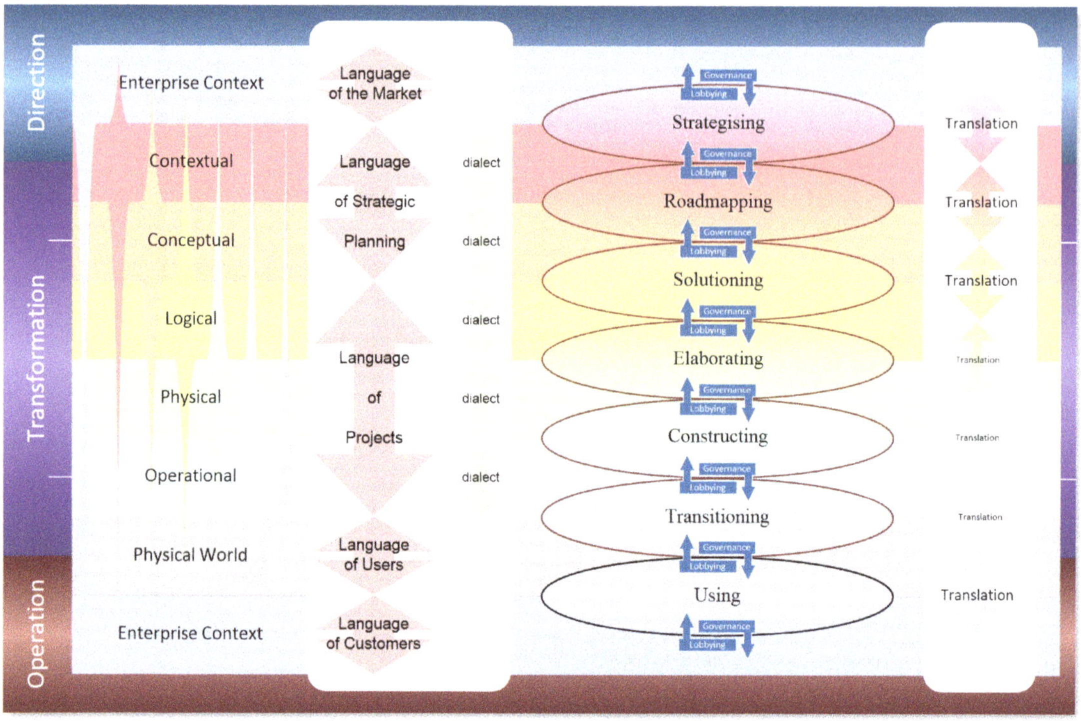

Although we all speak our native tongue fluently, the same cannot be said about the language we use to talk about things in relation to the Transformation of Enterprises. Different people use different words to mean different things at different times. This is a massive problem which makes understanding anything anyone says at best impossible and at worst apparently possible. People, including me, get attached to the meaning of the words we use and defend those meanings passionately. This is totally understandable because the meanings we attach to words is the absolute basis for our understanding things.

It is therefore extremely pertinent to understand how roles communicate with other roles at the same level, between levels in the same area and between each area. Languages correspond to the overall areas of The Market, Strategic Planning, Projects, Users and Customers. People within those areas can use slightly different words but they are more akin to dialects. Recognition of these different languages and dialects is important but more importantly is the realisation that people who operate in the various phases of the Transformation Stack need to be able to speak at least two different languages (if not three) and therefore also need to be able to translate between them depending on who they are talking to or what information they are dealing with.

There are five fundamental languages:

- **The Language of The Market** - The language used by senior executives and the board to communicate with The Enterprise Context (Regulators, Investors, Competitors, Suppliers, Customer Segments, Communities, Governments, Non-clients, Non Suppliers, Anti-Clients, The Media, etc)
- **The Language of Strategic Planning** - The language used by senior executives and the board to formulate the Enterprise Strategy as it relates to the Enterprise Context, and to create Strategic Plans, Project Portfolios and Roadmaps to execute any Transformation required to deliver the Strategy.

- **The Language of Projects** - The language used by all those working on Transformation projects while executing individual projects.
- **The Language of the Users** - The language used by those operating parts of the Enterprise that Transformation is delivered into.
- **The Language of Customers** - The Language used by those operating the business to relate to and communicate with Customers.

It is particularly important to pay attention to Governance and Lobbying where the fundamental Language barriers are. If the people performing those functions do not understand each others language, the whole Governance and Lobbying discipline will break down, and take the rest of the Transformation capability with it.

One thing a Framework or Ontology brings (hopefully!) is a common and consistent language. The importance of which should not be underestimated.

KEYPOINT:

For each phase of the Transformation cascade, people speak either a different dialect or language from the phases above and below.

ADOPTION:

C-Suite: Instigate an initiative to educate people on the different languages used in all areas of the Enterprise.

Questions to Ponder

- What Languages does your Enterprise use for Enterprise Transformation?
- Do people recognise when they are talking a different language?
- What happens when people say "we are talking a different language"?
- Are different languages taught?
- If not, how do you expect people to be able to communicate effectively?

Culture > Organisation Structure > Traditional vs Pragmatic

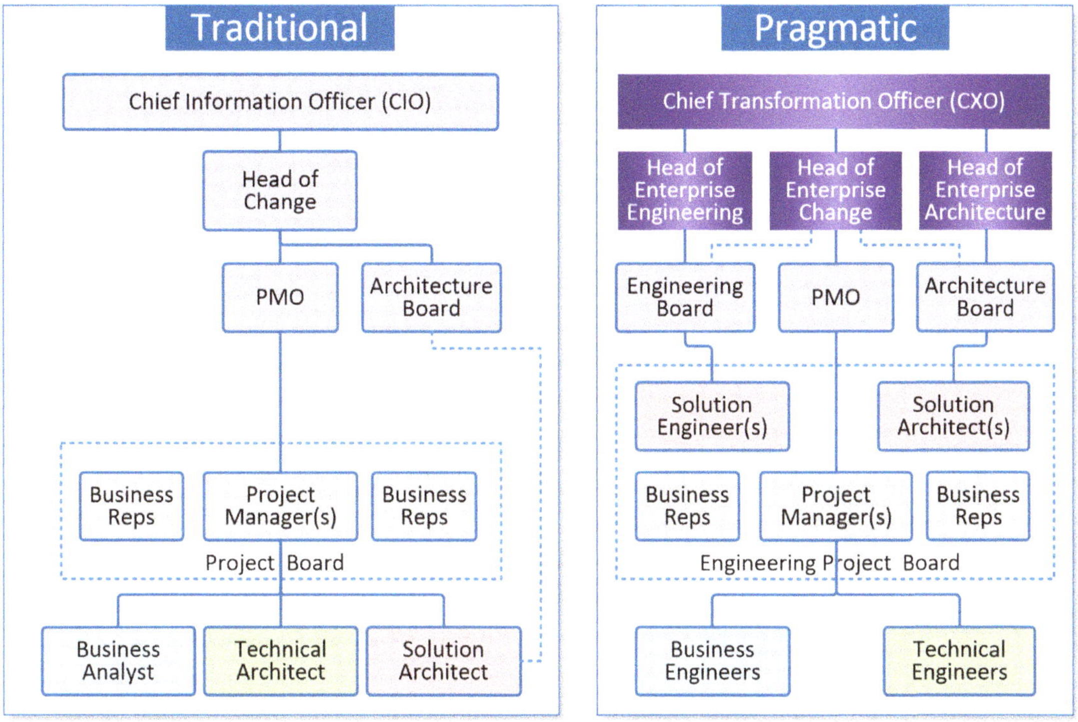

Although Enterprise Architecture has more to do with Roadmapping than Project Execution, EA still has a role on projects and that is one of Governance & Lobbying. Since much damage can be inflicted upon an Enterprise by how Projects execute, EA also has a remit to make sure the relationships in "projectland" work together cohesively.

Traditional Model

Any project today tends to be run with three key roles. The names may change from Enterprise to Enterprise or from country to country but broadly speaking these three roles exist:

- The **Business Analyst** is accountable for the Functional Fitness for purpose, takes Functional Requirements as input, and produces a Changed processes and provision of a functional capability as output.
- The **Technical Architect** is accountable for the Technical fitness for purpose, takes Non-Functional Requirements as input, and produces a Operating hardware and software as output.
- The **Solution Architect** is accountable for the whole logical design of the solution, taking the Conceptual Designs produce by Enterprise Architects as input and produces a Logical Solution Design as output.
- The **Project Manager** is accountable for the Project Budget and Deadlines, takes a Project Plan as input and produces a Completed Project as output.

Traditional

In the traditional model usually found in most Enterprises, the relationships are usually dysfunctional.

In spite of these dysfunctional relationships (which is at the expense of the Enterprise as a whole) things tend not to change because the people with the power required to change them are usually the ones that are incentivised to perpetuate them.

The SA, BA and TA "report" to the PM, with the PM being "in charge". The PM's voice is the loudest and tends to overrule the SA, BA and TA most (99%) of the time. This creates fundamental and important (negative) implications, but since the PM is not measured on any of them, he doesn't really care. And why should he, if that is how he is driven. This is normal and understandable, because everyone agrees that most projects these days run over time, budget etc, etc and therefore we need a "good" hard PM to keep everyone in check and make sure the project hits its budgets and timescales.

It is strange therefore that given this structure most projects fail.

The truth is that while this "power structure" is imposed to ensure projects complete on time and on budget, it is precisely this structure that causes them to fail. Doh!

The fundamental problem in the Traditional model, is that the work of the Solution Architect can discover significant problems or opportunities that could fundamentally change the project, other projects or even the Enterprise Architecture in operation. The Solution Architect must go to his boss (the PM) and try to convince him to either:

- Remove work from his project and put it in another existing project, then make his project dependent upon that project.
    - This never happens because PM's do not like being dependent on other things that could influence the success (time and budget) of their project.
- Remove work from another project and put it in his project, then make the other project dependent upon his project.
    - This never happens because PM's do not like having extra work added to their project that could influence the success (time and budget) of their project.
- Remove work from his project and put it in a new project, then make his project dependent upon that project.
    - This never happens because a) starting a new project requires a full cost/benefit analysis to be done and the project portfolio and budgets have already been agreed and cannot be changed and b) because PM's do not like being dependent on other things that could influence the success (time and budget) of their project.

And so, many serious problems, that could be fixed, are ignored and the project fails, while the PM and management still say it succeeded.

Alternatively, the unsolved problems cause so much knock-on effect that the project has to extend its deadlines and ask for more budget, while the PM and management still say it succeeded.

Alternatively, un-grasped opportunities do not make the savings or benefits they could have, while the PM and management still say it succeeded.

Alternatively, all of the above.

Pragmatic Model

In the **Pragmatic** model, the work of Solution Architecture (5-10% of most projects overall budget?) is taken out of projects. Projects therefore become Engineering projects and do not even start until the work of the Solution Architect is nearing completion.

In this way, all the problems identified in the Traditional Model (and witnessed by be on every single project I ever worked on as a Solution Architect over 20 years) are solved. All fundamental architectural concerns, problems and opportunities are ironed out without the hindrance of Project Managers.

In addition, we have renamed Business Analysts to Business Engineers because Business Analysts do not only Analyse, they also Design, largely at the physical level (composition/decomposition is used extensively, and composition/decomposition is not architecture). We have also renamed Technical Architects to be Technical Engineers because a) they are largely dealing with physical designs not logical designs and b) the Architecture title is given to many very experienced engineers, and c) to match the Business Engineer moniker.

KEYPOINT:

Solution Architecture is too important to be owned by Projects.

ADOPTION:

Management: Move Solution Architects work out of projects.

Questions to Ponder

- Does your Enterprise have SAs reporting to PMs?
- Does it create any problems?
- If so, what do you need to do to solve them?
- Do your Project Boards hear from the PM and SA or just the PM?
- If not does this cause any problems or issues?
- If so, what do you need to do to solve them?

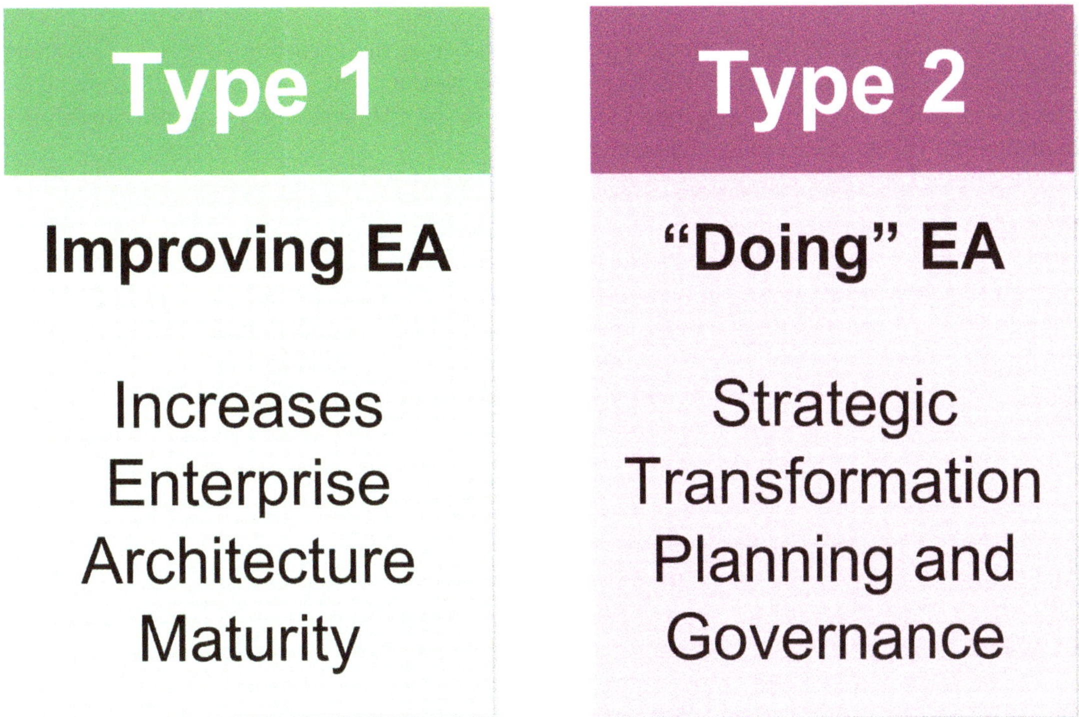

There are two types of Enterprise Architects:

- **Type 1** - This type of EA is responsible for increasing an Enterprises Maturity in its use of EA.
- **Type 2** - This type of EA is responsible for "doing" Enterprise Architecture.

Most (99.999%) Enterprises only ever recruit for a Type 2 Enterprise Architect - and therein lies the problem...

Whilst the job of the Type 2 EA is massively important and the things they produce are of massive benefit to the Enterprise, they are, in most cases, severely limited by the context of MAGIC that they are forced to work within.

But I hear you cry:

> "A good workman never blames his tools"

This is a common saying ("tools" = "context") and does have some validity.

However, it is also true to say that if you force a surgeon to:

- Save money – by not washing his hands before an operation (**Immature Methods**),
- Save money – by using untested blood and medicine (**Immature Artefacts**).
- Save money – by not following the guidance of the GMC (**Immature Guidance**).
- Save money – by using carving knife instead of a scalpel (**Immature Items**).
- Save money – by not living the Hippocratic Oath (**Immature Culture**).

You can hardly complain when patients keep dying.

Stopping patients dying is not achieved by replacing the Surgeon with another surgeon operating (no pun intended!) in the same context. Stopping patients dying is achieved by improving the Methods, Artefacts, Guidance, Items and Culture that they are forced to work within.

It is not in the Surgeon's power to increase the maturity of the Methods, Artefacts, Guidance, Items and Culture that surgeons are forced to work within, that is the job of Management - either with the guidance of Surgeons (hopefully!!) or by Management giving the Surgeons a mandate and resources to do so themselves.

I say hopefully because the National Health Service (NHS) in the UK demonstrates time and time again Management's utter lack of involving and listening to people who actually do the work regarding how to increase its maturity. But this is only one sad example of a much bigger cultural problem which exists all over the world today. A culture which effectively says, that people who are more senior are the ones who somehow magically know how to improve things. This used to be the case many decades ago when the Manager did know everything because he did the job himself for 40 years before he became the Manger, but in the 21st century Managers do not get appointed on that basis. They get appointed for all manner of strange reasons, all of which do nothing to help them actually do their job properly.

As we have said before, every Enterprise is already "doing" EA (operating on patients), it's just a question of their maturity in **How** they do it.

And in the same way that a surgeon cannot improve his context without a mandate, the same is true of a Type 2 EA. If the Type 2 EA's job description does not give him a mandate to increase maturity, then he is doomed to work within the constraints of his predecessor and almost certainly produce the same results. This always seems to come as a complete shock to Management who then blame that EA and go recruiting for a "better" one. Doh!

What is happening is that Management (because of Cognitive Dissonance) is actually ignoring the fundamental problem - which is themselves!

> "We have seen the enemy, and the enemy is us!"
>
> **- *W.E.Deming***

We could also say:

> "A good manager never blames"

KEYPOINT:

Recognise that there are two types of EA: 1. Those that improve how EA is done. 2. Those that "do" EA (Strategic Transformation Planning and Governance).

ADOPTION:

Management: Ensure everyone in the Enterprise understands that there are two types of Enterprise Architect.

Questions to Ponder

- Does your Enterprise recognize these two types of EA?
- How much time is spent on the duties of Type 1 vs Type 2?
- If you spent more time improving EA, would that reduce the amount of time spent "Doing" EA?

Culture > Enterprise Architect > Type 1 > Requirements

Purpose	Works With	Term
Helps an Enterprise to increase their EA maturity	Executive Management and the EA Team	Typically transitory / consultant
Focus	**Qualitites**	**Behaviours**
Communication, guiding and mentoring	Pragmatic, Enthusiastic, Agnostic, Articulate, Persistent, Strategic, Altruistic, Diplomatic, Open, Generalist.	Persuade, Learn, Investigate, Abstract, Expose, Facilitate, Lead.
EA Experience	**Business Experience**	**IT EA Experience**
Detailed	General	General

It is possible for one person to fulfil both roles (if given the mandate to do so), however, they are different in some fundamental respects.

The Type I Enterprise Architect's main role is not to "do" EA but to increase an Enterprises maturity in its use of EA - to ultimately allow those who "do" EA to be more effective and efficient.

This type of EA does not need any detailed business or IT knowledge, but they do need detailed knowledge about the EA profession, EA Frameworks and how to increase an Enterprise's EA maturity. That can come from their own innate knowledge and experience (a framework - even though it doesn't have a name and is not written down), from a published framework such as PEAF, or more likely a mixture of the two.

They can work in any type of Enterprise and can be equally as effective. It doesn't matter to a Type I EA whether the Enterprise is a bank, an oil company, a medical centre, the tax office, a university, an aircraft manufacturer, a hotel, an online retailer or a dog grooming company.

How transformation is effected and how its maturity can be increased is independent of the type of Enterprise. How Transformation is effected and the approach to the Transformation of Transformation is the same. What will ultimately be transformed (the Enterprise) can be very different but How transformation is effected is fundamentally the same irrespective of the type of Enterprise.

This type of EA therefore, is not an expert in your Enterprises Operations. They are (should be) an expert in the Enterprise called Transformation - that exists within all Enterprises. When interviewing for this type of person it is futile to ask questions such as "How much Banking Experience do you have".

KEYPOINT:

Type I Enterprise Architects help an Enterprise to increase their EA maturity.

ADOPTION:

Management: Ensure everyone in the Enterprise understands what a type I EA does.

Questions to Ponder

- Do you agree with these basic requirements for a Type I EA?
- If not, what would you change?

Strategising	Evangelise the benefits of EA. Expose the fundamental problem and opportunity and propose the fundamental solution.
Roadmapping	Evangelise the benefits of EA. Work with the EA project board to select an EA framework.
Solutioning	Evangelise the benefits of EA. Train the EA Team in the selected Framework. Work with the EA Team to a) articulate the EA vision and gain buy in from business and IT leaders across the organisation. b) define the EA Risks and mitigation strategies
Elaborating	Support the EA Team to a) Document the organisation's current EA maturity, b) define a target maturity level and the benefits of attaining that level, c) define a detailed implementation plan
Constructing	Support the EA Team to a) mitigate the risks, b) define the target Methods, Artefacts, Guidance, Items and Culture, c) define the transition plan
Transitioning	Support the EA Team to rollout the changes to the Methods, Artefacts, Culture and Items

The Type 1 EA is involved in Transformation. Not the Transformation of Operations (What the Type 2 does) but the Transformation of Transformation.

As such he also follows the standard Transformation phases of Strategising, Roadmapping, Solutioning, Elaborating, Construction and Transitioning, but these phases should not be confused with the phases in the context of the work a Type 2 EA does. For example, the Type 1 Roadmapping work is not concerned with creating the Roadmaps of the Enterprise, it is concerned with the roadmap to increase the Enterprise's Maturity in its use of EA.

Hence the phases we refer to here are the phases of the maturation of the EA capability.

KEYPOINT:

Type 1 Enterprise Architect's work, is primarily to; 1) Evangelise the benefits of EA. 2) Support the internal EA Team to mature how EA is performed.

ADOPTION:

Management: Ensure everyone in the Enterprise understands what a Type 1 Primary Tasks are.

Questions to Ponder

- Does anyone in your Enterprise perform these duties?
- If not, who will perform them?
- Are there people in your Enterprise already capable of performing these duties?
- If not, where will you get them from?

Culture > Enterprise Architect > Type 2 > Requirements

Purpose	Works With	Term
Strategic Transformation Planning and Governance	Strategic planning team & EA Steering Group	Typically permanent
Focus	**Qualitites**	**Behaviours**
Transformation Planning and Governance	Pragmatic, Enthusiastic, Agnostic, Articulate, Persistent, Strategic, Altruistic, Diplomatic, Open, Generalist.	Persuade, Learn, Investigate, Abstract, Expose, Facilitate, Lead.
EA Experience	**Business Experience**	**IT EA Experience**
General	Deatiles	Detailed

The Type 2 Enterprise Architect's main role is "do" EA for which he/she needs detailed (architecturally) Business and IT knowledge.

They need to really understand whatever the primary business role of the Enterprise is (be it a bank, an oil company, a medical centre, the tax office, a university, an aircraft manufacturer, a hotel, an online retailer or a dog grooming company) but also the Enterprise Context that that Enterprise Operates within.

They also need to really understand the place of IT within the Enterprise but also in the Enterprise Context in terms of vendors, products, services and technologies - both old, existing and upcoming - as part of their job is to highlight Technology Catalysts where a particular vendor, product, service or technology is exposed to the senior business executives that might provide competitive advantage.

KEYPOINT:

Type 2 Enterprise Architects do Strategic Transformation planning.

ADOPTION:

Management: Ensure everyone in the Enterprise understands what a type 2 EA does.

Questions to Ponder

- Do you agree with these basic requirements for a Type 2 EA?
- If not, what would you change?

Strategising	Evangelise the benefits of EA. Contributing to the Enterprise Strategy (Business & IT). Supporting the modelling, structured description, and the relationships between the parts of the Enterprise Strategy (Business, Motivation & Capability models)
Roadmapping	Evangelise the benefits of EA, Creating the Enterprise Transformation Strategy (Current, target and intermediate Capability and Roadmap models). Lobbying up to Strategising Phase, highlighting missed problems and/or opportunities.
Solutioning	Governance down to Project Execution, ensuring strategic guidance is followed. Accepting Lobbying up from Projects when missed problems and/or opportunities are discovered by Projects
Elaborating	Supporting
Constructing	Supporting
Transitioning	Supporting

The Type 2 EA is involved in Transformation. Not the Transformation of Transformation (What the Type 1 does) but the Transformation of Operations (or Support or Direction).

As such he also follows the standard Transformation phases but is only concerned with the Strategising, Roadmapping and Solutioning phases and the Governance and Lobbying between them. He may be required to participate in subsequent phases but only usually when there is a panic or specific strategic guidance is required.

KEYPOINT:

Type 2 Enterprise Architect's work, is primarily to; 1) support Strategising. 2) perform Roadmapping 3) Govern executing projects.

ADOPTION:

Management: Ensure everyone in the Enterprise understands what a Type 2 Primary Tasks are.

Questions to Ponder

- Does anyone in your Enterprise perform these duties?
- If not, who will perform them?
- Are there people in your Enterprise already capable of performing these duties?
- If not, where will you get them from?

"In many organizations, despite any rhetoric to the contrary, **people are rewarded for dealing with crises and problems**. The MVP is the one who came in at 3 a.m. to fix a problem, or who reacts instantly to the customer's complaint. Such an organization overlooks the fact that these MVP's are putting out fires that **either they set themselves and/or they failed to do anything to prevent**.

Then when we promote the MVP, **we wonder why nobody follows any processes** and everyone is always too overloaded to get anything right the first time. Why?

Because that is the behaviour that is rewarded."

- Douglas Brown (*Chief PMO - US Department of Defense)*

Here we see a very insightful quote from the Chief PMO of the US DoD.

It's something insidious, that happens within almost every Enterprise. Insidious because on the surface, it appears to be a laudable thing. Something to be celebrated. Who could say that a White Knight who rides in on a White Charger and saves the day, is a bad person?

But it's not the White Knight that is the problems. It is the environment (culture), that rewards people who put out fires but vilifies people who want o stop fires being started in the first place. And the culture is set by the management.

KEYPOINT:

While "firefighters" are always necessary, more resources need to be brought to bear as "fire prevention officers".

ADOPTION:

C-Suite: Reward those who prevent fires, as much as those that put them out.

Questions to Ponder

- How does your Enterprise reward people for dealing with crises and problems?
- How does your Enterprise reward people that try to prevent crises and problems?
- What will you do to change your Enterprise's approach?

- Personal Motivation
- Career Outlook
- Financial Motivation

Here we compare "The Management" and "The Workers" in various ways. Obviously the comparisons shown here will not apply to every Manager and every Worker in every Enterprise. For example, there will be managers who stay at one Enterprise the whole of their life, and there will be Workers that change jobs every two years. It is also accepted that there can be in many cases a blurring between "The Management" and "The Workers".

This section just highlights the general differences that can exist. Whether they do or not, and to what extent, will depend on each individual Enterprise.

You are invited to create your own depending upon the specifics of your Enterprise.

Personal Motivation

- Management
    - Short term.
    - Driven by challenge and money.
    - Know that they will probably not be around when any long term problems they create come to pass, and therefore concentrate solely on today's problems.
- The Workers
    - Long term.
    - Driven by stability and money.
    - Know that they will probably have to deal with any long term problems that are created and therefore try to "head them off at the pass" whenever they can by highlighting them to Management.

Career Outlook

- Management

- Generally look to move on to a different Enterprise every 2 or 3 years.
- They recognise that career development mostly comes from changing Enterprises and not from promotion within an Enterprise.
- A move to another Enterprise is seem as an exciting new challenge.

- The Workers
  - Generally look for stability and to stay at one Enterprise for long periods.
  - Things have to get pretty bad before they do anything about changing Enterprises.
  - A move to another Enterprise is seen as a worrying and disrupting event.

Financial Motivation

- Management
  - Short Term.
  - Bonuses based on this year's achievements and paid almost immediately.
- The Workers
  - Long Term.
  - Bonuses based on this year's achievements and usually paid over long periods to avoid the possibility that large numbers of employees will leave after they get their bonus.

KEYPOINT:

You cannot change what you don't understand and you cannot understand what you cannot see.

ADOPTION:

EA Project Team: Model the culture between the Management and Workers.

Questions to Ponder

- In which ways would you compare "The Management" vs "The Workers"?
- How does the personal motivation of "The Management" and "The Workers" in your Enterprise compare?
- How does the career outlook of "The Management" and "The Workers" in your Enterprise compare?
- How does the financial motivation of "The Management" and "The Workers" in your Enterprise compare?
- Does that create any tensions or problems or issues?
- What do you need to do to solve them?

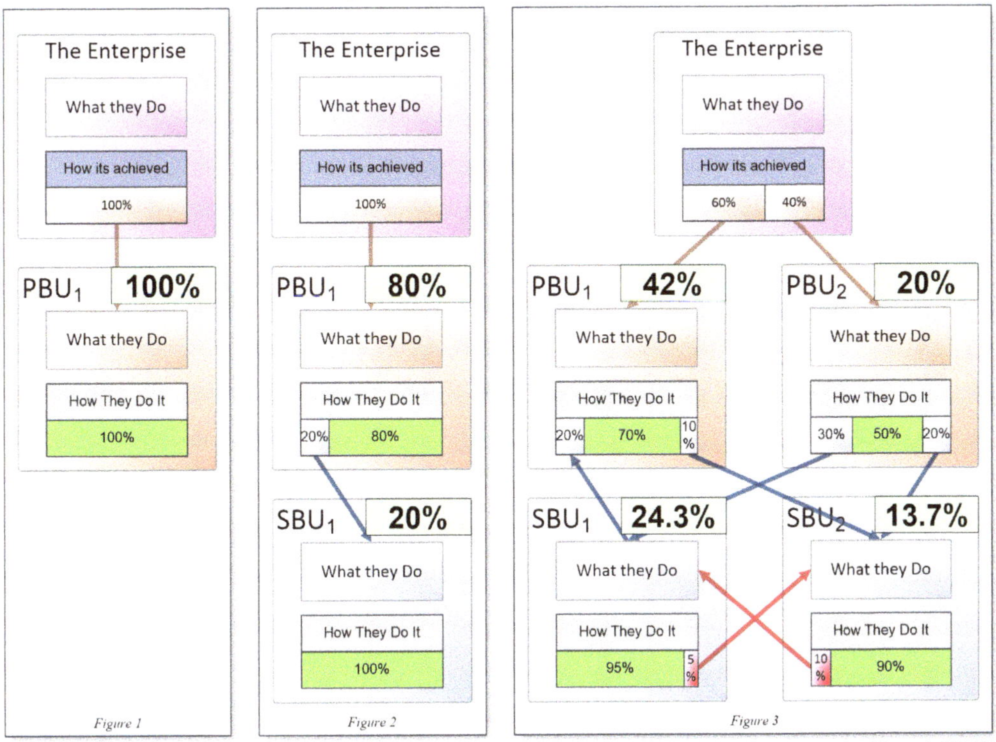

An Enterprise is split into various Business Units (BUs). Primary Business Units (PBUs) equate to those Business Units that perform the main role of the Enterprise such as Sales, Banking, Drilling oil wells, etc. Supporting Business Units (SBUs) are those which support the PBU's, usually supporting multiple PBU's

Each BU (be it Primary or Support) can be split into two fundamental notional parts.

- **What** they do - This relates to the business function they perform - be it selling things, drilling for oil, recruitment, training people, providing financial reports and auditing, etc.
- **How** they do it - This relates to how they perform their business function and with what.

Figure 1.

Here the Enterprise has one department - PBU_1.

100% of the **How** is work is carried out, is carried out by PBU_1.

Figure 2.

In a larger more complex Enterprise there may be another department - SBU_1.

While PBU_1 is still responsible for 100% of the **What**, it is now only performs 80% of the **How** - as the other 20% of the **How** is now carried out by SBU_1.

Figure 3.

An even more complex Enterprise may be structured as follows:

- PBU_1 is responsible for 60% of **How** the Enterprise achieves what they do.
- PBU_2 is responsible for 40% of **How** the Enterprise achieves what they do.

Considering PBU_1

- 20% of **How** it does what it does, is done by SBU_1
- 70% of **How** it does what it does, it does itself.
- 10% of **How** it does what it does, is done by SBU_2

Considering PBU_2

- 30% of **How** it does what it does, is done by the SBU_1
- 50% of **How** it does what it does, it does itself.
- 20% of **How** it does what it does, is done by SBU_2

Considering SBU_1

- 5% of **How** it does what it does, is done by SBU2
- 95% of **How** it does what it does, it does itself.

Considering SBU_2

- 10% of **How** it does what it does, is done by the SBU_1
- 90% of **How** it does what it does, it does itself.

On the face of it, PBU_1 looks like the most important BU and PBU_2 looks the second most important. However…

If we work out **How** each of the BUs contributes to doing the work necessary for the Enterprise, we can see that SBU_2 is actually the second most important BU, not PBU_2, in terms of **How** the Enterprise does what they do.

- PBU_1 is responsible for 42% of the **How**.
- PBU_2 is responsible for 20% of the **How**.
- SBU_1 is responsible for 24.3% of the **How**.
- SBU_2 is responsible for 13.7% of the **How**.

KEYPOINT:

HOW each part of your Enterprise does what they do, shows the real contribution toward achieving the Enterprises Mission.

ADOPTION:

C-Suite: Instigate an initiative to calculate how much each part of the Enterprise contributes to it's Mission.

Questions to Ponder

- Does your Enterprise consider what percentage each department contributes to what they do?
- How many PBUs and SBUs does your Enterprise have?
- What are their names and what are their relationships?

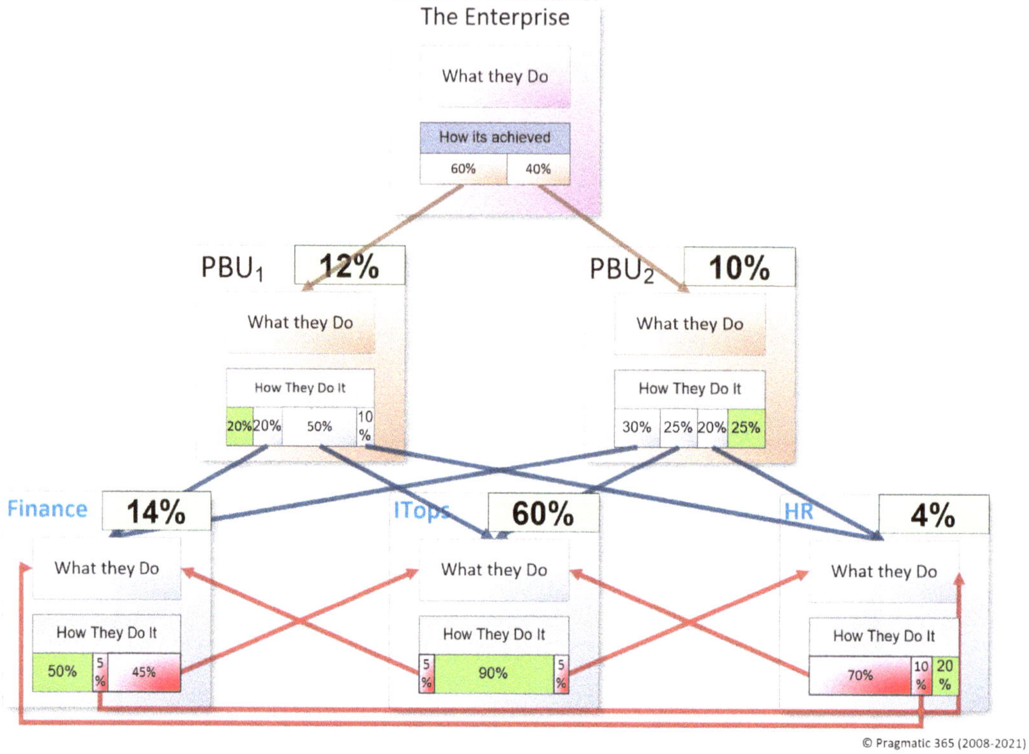

With a third SBU, we are beginning to approximate the complexity of many Enterprises today. We have also replaced the SBU monikers with representative names of Finance, IT and HR.

Essentially we are showing that a large proportion of How the PBUs do what they do, is done by IT. We are also showing that a large proportion of How Finance and HR do what they do, is also done by IT.

Given these percentages we can work out **How** each of the BUs contributes to doing the work necessary for the Enterprise.

(These figures are not entirely accurate because of the circular/recursive nature of them, however, they do illustrate the point, and it's not the accurate numbers that are important but the overall story the numbers are telling us.)

- PBU_1 is responsible for 12% of the **How**.
- PBU_2 is responsible for 10% of the **How**.
- Finance is responsible for 14% of the **How**.
- ITops is responsible for 60% of the **How**.
- HR is responsible for 4% of the **How**.

These percentages are not a reflection of the "importance" of each BU, nor do they reflect how much each BU contributes financially to the bottom line, however it is an important way to look at which areas do the most work. If ITops is doing 60% of the How, why would an Enterprises deem it to be a Cost centre rather than a Profit centre?

In a world before IT, no BU grew so much to completely dwarf other BUs because if it did, it is likely that it would have been divided up into more manageable PBUs or SBUs. When IT first began to be used by Enterprises, the IT BU was only responsible for a very low percentage of the overall **How**.

As time has gone by, the use of IT has grown and grown. More and more of the **How** was taken out of the BU where that work is done and wrapped up in IT systems. In many Enterprises this has now grown to such a point that in the example shown above where ITops is responsible for 60% of the **How**.

So, IT is a special case, but not because it's IT. IT is a special case because it is responsible for the majority of the **How** of an Enterprise.

KEYPOINT:

IT is special not because it is IT, but because IT tends to be responsible for a large part of HOW an Enterprise does what it does.

ADOPTION:

Management: Ensure everyone in the Enterprise understands that IT is special, but not because its IT.

Questions to Ponder

- Does the Leadership of your Enterprise understand how much IT contributes to the bottom line?
- Does your Enterprise treat IT Operations as a cost centre or a revenue stream?
- What percentages would apply to your Enterprise?
- Which PBU or SBU is responsible for most of the "How they do it" of your Enterprise?

Culture > IT vs "The Business" > When Two Tribes Go To War

© Pragmatic 365 (2008-2021)

In many Enterprises it may not necessarily be that IT and "The Business" are at war but in most they are most definitely two tribes. This does not necessarily mean there is a problem. It's OK to have two (or many) tribes. It only becomes a problem when one tribe seeks to control the other.

Even if you do not believe or accept that IT and the Business is at war, perhaps it's because it's more of a cold war.

Whatever the status within your Enterprise, the relationship between IT and "The Business" is one of monumental importance and therefore understanding that relationship and improving it should be a strategic aim of the Business.

A Marriage of Convenience

The relationship between IT and the rest of the Enterprise is usually one of uneasy bedfellows. In fact the relationship could be thought of like a marriage than anything else.

It starts out with huge amounts of love and positivity. The two cannot bear to be separated for more than 10 seconds at a time. But as time goes on, they can begin to start to see the cracks and the little annoyances.

Some marriages work well, some do not.

In marriage, one party can get so fed up they find another partner they do like and commit adultery. In Enterprises adultery is represented by parts of the Enterprise sourcing systems and IT for itself or using small consultancies under the wire, working directly for the rest of the Enterprise instead of through IT.

In marriage, when the relationship breaks down irrevocably there is divorce. In Enterprises divorce could be synonymous with outsourcing....which may lead to another marriage...

The thing to remember is that it all comes down to relationships (which basically is all about communication) and if people/groups are flawed in the way they approach relationships (e.g.

flawed in communication) it doesn't matter how many flings or divorces they have, they will always have relationships that fail. It's not a matter of if, but a matter of when.

> "Men are from Mars, Women are from Venus"
>
> "IT is from Mars, The Business is from Venus"

Mind the gap!

For a marriage to be successful both parties need to work on the relationship on a daily basis. Whether the marriage is between two people, two Enterprises or two groups within an Enterprise. That is why communication is the most important aspect of EA's tenet to "Bridge the gap between the rest of the Enterprise and IT".

In fact that oft used phrase is actually fundamentally flawed. Bridging the gap intimates that the two parts continue to be separate and that there is a gap which needs to be bridged.

EA will not, and does not bridge the gap.

EA helps to reduce and ultimately remove the gap.

There is only a slight change of words but the implications are profound.

Continuing the marriage analogy, you can think of Enterprise Architects (the people), Enterprise Architecture (the process) and Enterprise Architecture (the product) as a kind of marriage counsellor or mediator, helping both parties to find a way to get back in touch with each other. EA, like counselling, doesn't bring answers, it allow the parties to communicate in positive ways so they arrive at their own decisions about how they want to change.

KEYPOINT:

Recognise and deal with the fact that IT and The Business do constitute "Two Tribes".

ADOPTION:

C-Suite: Instigate an initiative to bring the two tribes (Business and IT) together.

Questions to Ponder

- Is your IT department at war with "The Business"?
- Do they work together in a coherent and holistic partnership?
- Are they somewhere in between?
- Does that create any tensions or problems or issues?
- What do you need to do to solve them?

Should IT ever say NO to "the business"?

IT should never say no.

EA does not make decisions.
EA is a facilitator.

IT should always say yes, but…
Pros, Cons, Costs, Risks, Implications.

Should IT ever say "No" to the Business?

In a word. NO! Or, to put it another way **NO. Never. Ever. NO!**

I know what you are thinking…

> "There will be sometimes when we (IT) just have to say no because what they want us to do is just plain wrong, illogical, stupid, crazy, etc, etc, etc. Like if they asked us to give all their customers a Tablet and expect us to maintain them, or if they asked us to remove all the backup storage, or if they told us to use COBOL instead of JAVA….."

The point is - who is to decide what is wrong, illogical, stupid, crazy, etc, etc, etc.

"The Business" will have access to much more information than IT and therefore IT will never be in a position to say what they are being asked to do is wrong, illogical, stupid, crazy, etc, etc, etc. From an IT persons perspective things may well look wrong, illogical, stupid or crazy but from the Business perspective things may look so obviously right that they find it hard to understand why IT is saying no and appearing to be trying to block things.

This does not, of course mean that IT will not have an opinion and may offer recommendations, but that is very different.

When IT starts to make decisions and therefore effectively refuses to do what the Business asks of it, it immediately puts IT in the role of a blocker, a problem, a difficult child, a loose cannon, a "difficult person". IT being seen in this light is a major major problem - for IT itself but more importantly for the entire Enterprise.

IT needs to understand its place (and especially the role of EA) is to make "The Business" aware of the implications of what they are asking IT to do. By doing so, IT forces "The Business" to take accountability for those decisions. If not, the IT department will continue to be its own worst enemy.

The business is in control of an Enterprise but many have lost control of the IT department. EA puts the business back in control of Enterprise Transformation, including the IT department, and at the same time allows the people in the IT department to sleep at night.

The caveat is, of course, if "The Business" bestows on IT the power to make certain decisions within specified limits. If this happens, it is still not IT making the decision. It is still the Business making the decision. IT is merely the messenger, and if problems accepting that decision come about, then it is ultimately the business whose responsibility it is to defend or change it.

> KEYPOINT:
>
> IT should never say "No" to the Business. It should say "Yes, but…".

> ADOPTION:
>
> Enterprise Architect: Don't ever say No to the Business.
>
> The Business: Own the implications of your requirements

Questions to Ponder

- Do people in your IT department ever say no to the business?
- Does that create any tensions or problems or issues?
- What do you need to do to solve them?

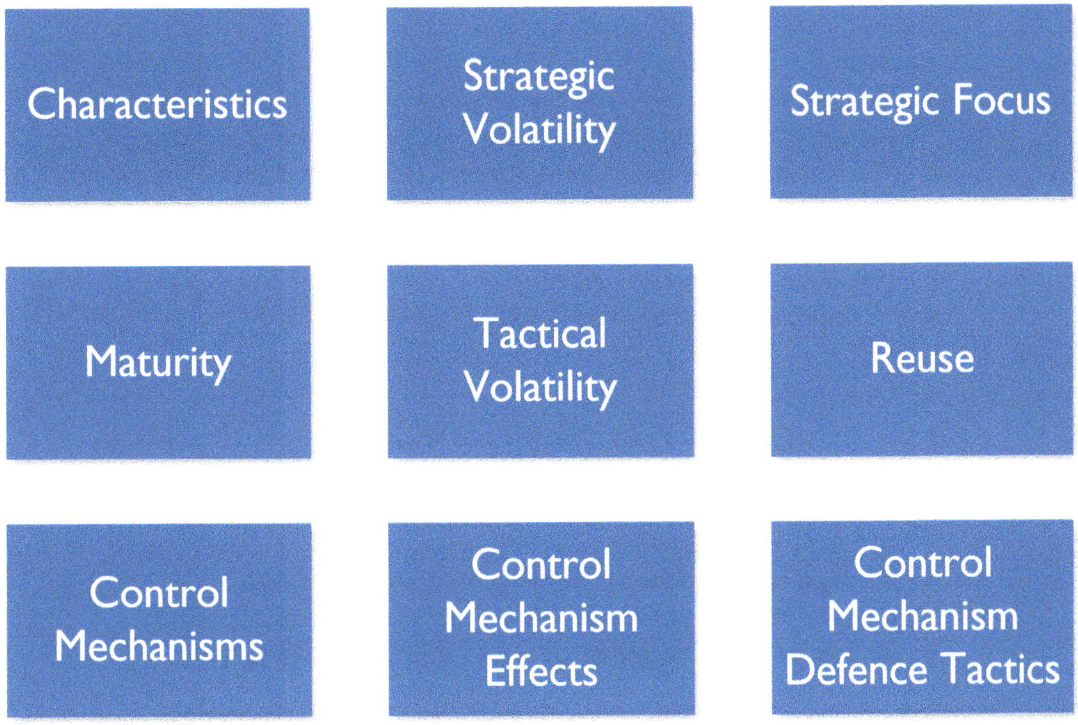

It is useful to analyse the differences between IT and the Business. These are, of course, generalities and need to be reviewed in light of each individual Enterprise.

Characteristics

- The Business
    - Analog.
    - Very grey - no rights or wrongs .
    - The Business don't want things to be black and white.
    - Grey is where opportunities lie.
    - Women - Venus - right brain - intuitive, thoughtful, subjective.
- IT
    - Digital
    - Very black and white - things work or they don't.
    - IT's ambition is to reduce the grey and increase the black and white.
    - Grey is where problems lie.
    - Men - Mars - left brain - logical, analytical, objective.

It in no way asserts that women cannot be logical, analytical or objective.

It in no way asserts that men cannot be intuitive, thoughtful or subjective.

Men and women are equal, but different. In the same way that an apple and an orange are equal but different.

The Business and IT are equal, but different. Instead of pretending they are the same, both sides need to understand the other to be able to work together in harmony. Like a marriage.

Strategic Volatility

- The Business
    - High.
    - Major strategic change/direction could occur at any time, e.g. legislative change, market opportunity, hostile takeover, acquisition opportunity.
    - The world is a fast moving environment. Businesses that don't react and react quickly tend to suffer at the hands of those that do.
    - Therefore The Business wants to be agile and definitely does not want to be tied into a fixed plan/strategy.
    - The Business likes things to be fluid and flexible.
- IT
    - Low.
    - IT Strategy doesn't really change much from year to year. Technology changes very fast but the IT Strategy tends to be reasonably stable.
    - The focus tends to be the same and tends to be focussed on cost reduction and service availability.
    - Strategic change can have a massive and detrimental effect on IT and The Business and there any large strategic changes tend to be avoided.
    - IT likes things well defined and locked down and prescriptive.

Strategic Focus

- The Business
    - Business Verticals - Banking, Manufacturing...
    - Increase Revenue- Sell more, acquisitions...
    - Decrease Costs - Use less, outsource, common services
- IT
    - IT Service Management - Availability, DR...
    - IT Project Management - On Time, to Budget...
    - IT Cost Reduction - Rationalisation, Outsourcing...
    - IT Planning - Architecture, Roadmaps, Governance...

Maturity

- The Business
    - Generally speaking other SBUs and the functions they perform have existed for hundreds of years and have generally not changed much.
    - The services they provide to PBUs and the SBU's are generally identical.
- IT
    - IT is a new kid on the block and as such is not as mature and standardised as the other SBUs.
    - The services IT provides to other SBUs have not changed much in function but have changed radically in how they are provided and implemented.
    - The services IT provides to PBUs have changed radically over generally short timeframes and have also changed in how they are provided and implemented.

Tactical Volatility

- The Business
    - Low or High - Small number of changes with potentially massive impact.
    - The Business may make tactical decisions at any time - these tactical decisions at The Business level (although 'simple') could have (or more likely are constrained by) massive changes required to effect the changes required, especially in IT.
- IT
    - High
    - Large number of changes to respond to every little change in the Enterprise.
    - Emphasis on reducing this - key to stopping this is to decouple.

Reuse

- The Business
    - Very low.
    - At a high level
    - The only common/ reused services are Locations, HR, Finance, Procurement and IT, etc, etc.
- IT
    - Very High.
    - At a low level.
    - Servers, databases, applications, data, components, racks, networks, workstations, builds, etc, etc.

Control Mechanisms

- The Business
    - The Business tries to control IT by limiting time, money, resources, the scope of projects or any combination thereof.
- IT
    - IT tries to control The Business by forcing it to be more and more prescriptive with the documentation of its strategies and project requirements.
    - IT also tries to control The Business by forcing projects to comply with a set of prescriptive IT principles, IT policies and IT standards.

Control Mechanism Effects

- The Business
    - The Business views IT as very inflexible and thinks IT is more interested in technology that The Business it is meant to support.
- IT
    - IT views The Business as meddling in their affairs and forcing them to do sub-standard work which The Business then blames IT for.
    - Projects over run timescales and budgets and do not provide the services The Business requires.

Control Mechanism Defence Tactics

- The Business

    - The Business knows that IT will always want more money and time and therefore restricts time and money as a defence tactic.
- IT
    - IT knows that The Business will always restrict time and money and therefore inflates project estimates to "counter the cuts".

KEYPOINT:

You cannot change what you don't understand and you cannot understand what you cannot see.

ADOPTION:

Enterprise Architect: Model the culture between IT and "The Business".

Questions to Ponder

- How does The Business and IT compare in your Enterprise?
- Does that create any tensions or problems or issues?
- What do you need to do to solve them?

Culture > Roles > Overview

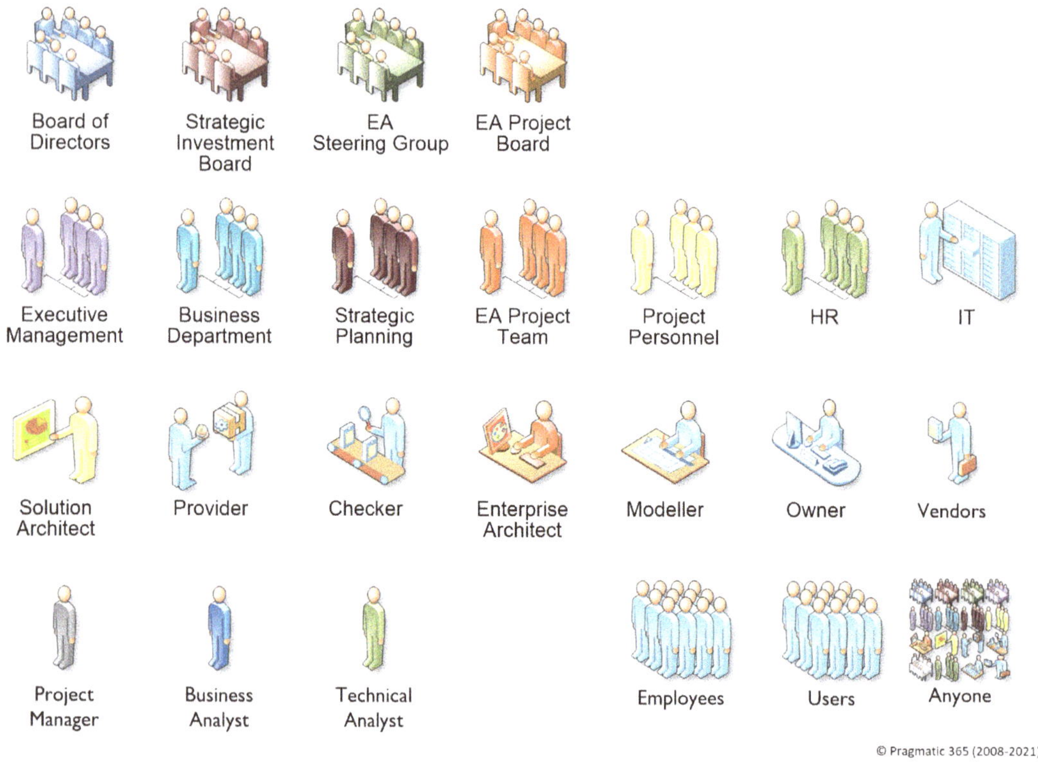

The following table details the graphics used to represent people or groups shown on the PEAF process diagrams.

Boards

Board of Directors (BOD)
The Statutory company board of directors for limited companies or for government bodies/agencies, the group of individuals responsible for setting policy and direction.

Strategic Investment Board (SIB)
A group, with budget, that can decide, or not, to provided extra time, money, people, scope to projects if it would create strategic benefit or competitive advantage.

EA Steering Group (EASG)
A group with powers devolved from the SIB and the BOD which ensures that solutions conform, where appropriate, to strategic principles and roadmaps and ensures that Transformation Debt™ is uncovered and documented.

EA Project Board (EAPB)
The project board of the EA Implementation project.

Groups

Executive Management
The Enterprise wide group of people responsible for turning the Enterprise strategy into reality and managing all work undertaken.

Business Department
Any department in the Enterprise playing a primary business role.
(i.e. Any department not playing a supporting business role)

Strategic Planning
The group of people responsible for annual business planning and the formulation of Business and IT Strategy to support the Enterprise Strategy.

EA Project Team
The group of people tasked with increase the Enterprise maturity in its use of Enterprise Architecture.

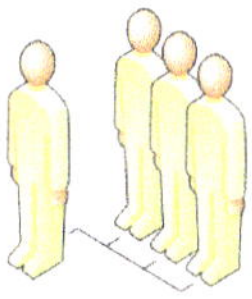

Project Personnel
Anyone working on a project. e.g. Project Mangers, Business Analysts, Architects, Developers, etc.

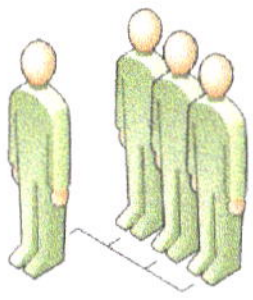

Human Resources (HR)

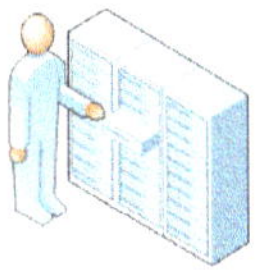

Information Technology (IT)

Employees

Users

Enterprise Architect - Type 1 (Increasing EA maturity)
Enterprise Architect - Type 2 ("doing" EA)

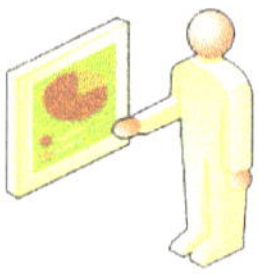

Solution Architect

Vendor

Provider (Modelling)

This role is Responsible for finding and extracting the information from wherever it currently resides and providing a consolidated set of information to the Checker and tends to be the people who currently use this information.

This role will almost certainly be fulfilled by people already working for Enterprise.

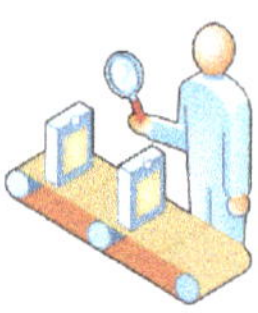

Checker (Modelling)

This role is Responsible for analysing the information and making sure that all the information collected is consistent and correct.
This role will almost certainly be fulfilled by team leaders and managers already working for the Enterprise.

Modeller (Modelling)

This role is Responsible for taking the Quality Controlled information provided by the SME and entering it into the modelling tool.

This role could be fulfilled by individuals already working for the Enterprise (having received appropriate training) or equally could be fulfilled by the tool vendor's professional services team.

Owner (Modelling)

This role is Accountable for keeping the information in the model up to date, consistent and correct.

KEYPOINT:

PEAF refers to various roles, most of which will already exist in an Enterprise.

ADOPTION:

EA Project Team: Map Pragmatic Roles to your Enterprise's roles.

Questions to Ponder

- Do these roles exist within your Enterprise?
- Are they called the same names?
- Which ones are missing?

Purpose

Release more resources (people, time, money, increased scope, etc) where it is in the best interests of the whole enterprise to do so

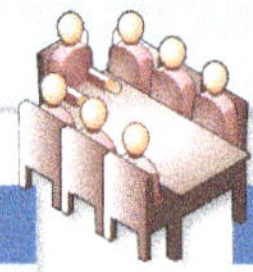

SIB

Budget Holding

Strategic Investment Budget

Escalation Route

None

Permanent Members

- Business Directors
- CTO/CIO/IT Director
- Enterprise Architect

Transient Members

- Project Managers
- Solution Architects
- Business Analysts

KEYPOINT:

An SIB with allocated budget and power is mandatory for Governance & Lobbying to operate effectively.

ADOPTION:

EA Project Team: Create a Strategic Transformation Investment Board (SIB) with allocated budget and power.

Questions to Ponder

- Does your Enterprise have an SIB?
- If not, does it create any problems?
- If so, what do you need to do to solve them?

Culture > Roles > EASG (Enterprise Architecture Steering Group)

Purpose

Ensure that solutions conform where possible to strategic principles and roadmaps. Ensure that cross projects synergies are exploited where possible. Ensure that all Transformation Debt™ is exposed. Request more resources (people, time, money increased scope) where it is in the best interests of the enterprise to do so

EASG

Budget Holding

Delegated from the Strategic Investment Board

Escalation Route

Strategic Investment Board

Permanent Members

- Enterprise Architect
- Head of Business Change
- Business SMEs
- Head of IT Development
- Head of IT Operations

Transient Members

- Project Managers
- Solution Architects
- Business Analysts

The Enterprise Architecture Steering Group {{James McGovern}} exists to guide the execution of Transformation as it progresses, and to ensure that any deviations from roadmaps, principles or policies are recognised, understood and evaluated.

KEYPOINT:

An EASG with delegated budget and power is mandatory for Governance & Lobbying to operate effectively.

ADOPTION:

EA Project Team: Create an Enterprise Architecture Steering Group.

Questions to Ponder

- Does your Enterprise have an EASG?
- Does it hold delegated budgetary responsibility from the SIB?
- Does it have an escalation route to the SIB?
- If not, does it create any problems?
- If so, what do you need to do to solve them?

APPENDIX

KEYPOINT:

The Appendix section contains information on the background of PF2, POET, PEAF and the author.

WHY?	• We Care About Enterprises • We Care About the People who Direct, Operate, Transform and Support Enterprises
WHEN?	• PEAF 2008 • POET 2014 • PTMC 2018
WHERE?	• Born from Observing Failure
HOW?	• 150,000 Hours of Thinking • 20,000 Hours of Creating
USING WHAT?	• Architecture, Engineering, Altruism • Honesty, Integrity, Persistence, Passion • Common Sense, Logic

Why Were They Created?

Because I care. Because I care about Enterprises. Because I care about the people who **Direct**, **Operate**, **Transform** and **Support** Enterprises. Because I am angry about how much time is wasted. Because I am angry about how much money is wasted. From the Afghani to the Zloty, I guarantee you are wasting it. Big time!

This work was inspired by all those who seek to make the world a better place rather than those that seek to own it.

When Were They Created?

PEAF was initially launched in November 2008 and POET in 2014.

Where Did They Come From?

All **Pragmatic** Ontologies and Frameworks were created from observing failure. That is:

- Seeing why people fail
- What problems they encounter
- Providing things to reduce the risk of others failing in the same way
- Providing things to alleviate the problems people have.

Around 2002 I began to be interested in something called "Enterprise Architecture". The term started to appear more in publications and people started to talk about it more - although from listening to them there never seemed to be a concrete definition of what it actually was that everyone agreed with (some say that's still the case today!). Using logic and common sense I could surmise that it was not Project level Architecture (because that already had a name -

Solution Architecture) and therefore it must be something at a "higher level" - not just bigger. Something related to:

- What goes on before projects execute and before Solution Architects start working on those projects.
- Enterprise Centric, or more specifically Enterprise Transformation Centric, rather than Project Centric and/or IT Centric.

At that time it all seemed to be a bit of a black art (some say it still is!) and so, being an Architect and not wanting to reinvent the wheel (others call it being lazy!), I surmised that there must be something out there (a bit like Prince or ITIL or MSP for example) - a framework - that might help people to "do" EA by:

- Helping people understand what EA was.
- Helping people increase the maturity in how an Enterprise "does" EA.

So, I consulted the mighty Google (sorry Oracle!). Google told me about something called Zachman and something called TOGAF. And so I went off to investigate further.

From what I could tell, Zachman's message seemed to resonate well with me in terms of general thinking I had built up over the preceding 20 years, namely:

- You can't change what you can't see - hence the need to model things - in a structured way.
- There must be Phases involved in Transformation to get from Strategic intent at the top down to real physically deployed things at the bottom.

These basic messages haven't changed and are as valid today as they always were - although the important distinction between Enterprise Architecture and Enterprise Engineering that **Pragmatic** makes today was not (and still is not) recognised in Zachman (despite my attempts to do so). But, whilst these fundamental things (modelling and phases/levels) were a good start, they were much too high level to provide any practical help in using them (which is what a framework is supposed to do) and so I invested more time looking into the much more detailed TOGAF.

As I looked into TOGAF, the first thing that struck me was "Where the hell do I start?". The material was immense, complex, confusing, very dry, hard to consume and offered no guidance about how to adopt it. So, assuming it was my ignorance that was the problem I booked myself on a TOGAF course. Within the first 2 hours of the first day it became clear that it was centred around Project level IT centric Architecture.

Nothing wrong with Project level IT centric Architecture, but not Enterprise Architecture.

Fantastic for those Enterprises that had still not figured out that the complexity of the IT landscape had grown to such a level that using Architecture as a discipline on IT Projects (Solution Architecture) was almost mandatory (unless you wanted to waste a shed load of money and deliver a shed load of bad IT to customers), but not Enterprise Architecture.

Great for those Enterprise that wanted to formalise their Solution Architecture discipline, but not Enterprise Architecture.

Great for those Enterprises that wanted to continue to treat "The Business" as a second class citizen to "IT", but not Enterprise Architecture.

At least not the Enterprise Architecture that logic and common sense dictated to me.

Anyway, I got through the course, passed the exams and became TOGAF Certified. Over the next few years I worked at various organisations and my TOGAF certification served me well in terms of getting me job interviews and most of the subsequent contracts. Having got a contract (because I was TOGAF certified) I then endeavoured to first discover how much and what parts of TOGAF were being used. The conversation (over many days, sometimes weeks) usually went something like this:

> K: "Hi Allen, I'm new here. I've been told that you use TOGAF, can you tell me what parts you are using and which you aren't?"
> A: "Hi Kevin, Errrmm, Yeah sure - you need to talk to Steve, he's the one that did the training."

<time passes....>

> K: "Hi Steve, I'm new here. I've been told that you use TOGAF, can you tell me what parts you are using and which you aren't?"
> S: "Hi Kevin, Errrmm, why are you asking me?"
> K: "Allen told me you did the training and you would know."
> S: "Err yeah, but I was only one of the twenty people who did it, I wasn't the main person. Listen - I'm a bit busy on this CRM project at the moment, can you go and ask James about it - I think he was the main guy."

<time passes....>

> K: "Hi James, I'm new here. I've been told that you use TOGAF, can you tell me what parts you are using and which you aren't?"
> J: "Hi Kevin, Errrmm, why are you asking me?"
> K: "Steve told me you did the training and you were the main guy so you would know."
> J: "Err yeah, but I was moved off that onto this ESB project. Listen - I'm a bit busy at the moment, Dave took over that TOGAF thing - go talk to Dave."

<time passes....>

> K: "Hi Dave, I'm new here. I've been told that you use TOGAF, can you tell me what parts you are using and which you aren't?"
> D: "Hi Kevin, Errrmm - why are you asking me?"
> K: "James told me you did the training and you're now the guy in charge of TOGAF adoption."
> D: "Err No! That's Chris, you need to talk to Chris"

<time passes....>

> K: "Hi Chris, I'm new here. I've been told that you use TOGAF, can you tell me what parts you are using and which you aren't?"
> C: "Hi Kevin, Errrmm, why are you asking me?"
> K: "James told me Dave did the training and he was the guy in charge of TOGAF adoption, but that Dave says it wasn't him, it was you"

> C: "Err Yeah - well I went on the course, but to be honest we never did anything about if after that, you should go talk to Allen, he knows what's going on"

In every case, after being passed from pillar to post, it always transpired that no one was actually using TOGAF at all.

So, I began to build up my own intellectual capital (documents, checklists, presentations, spreadsheets, ideas, concepts, processes, products, etc) so that I could bring them to bear as a set of quick start artefacts for subsequent contracts.

During 2008 it suddenly dawned on me that all this intellectual capital that I had built up, actually constituted what I thought an EA framework should contain. So, in addition to cleaning up and structuring the material so others could adopt and use it easily, I had to choose a name. So, I thought, what one word would sum up my approach? A core of fundamental things - the 20% that would give 80% of the benefit - that would reduce or remove 20% of the risks that cause 80% of the failures. Cutting through all the smoke and mirrors and Cutting EA to the Bone. And so the name **Pragmatic** chose me.

How Were They Created?

POET and PEAF have taken more than 10,000 hours to produce in terms of physical work, born from approximately 150,000 hours of thinking. The graphics were not just drawn - like most good things they evolved - and while many of them look quite simple, it took an awful lot of work and pain to get to those simple graphics. To an outside observer, those diagrams could appear as if someone just sat down and drew them but each one has had many versions as it has evolved, coalesced, fragmented, reconstituted, gone down the wrong track, fragmented, coalesced again and then finally thrown away, only to be resurrected when a light bulb went on somewhere in the deepest darkest recesses of my feeble brain.

Elegance and simplicity takes a lot of hard work to achieve but, anything **Pragmatic** must be so.

> "Je n'ai fait celle-ci plus longue que parce que je n'ai pas eu le loisir de la faire plus courte."
>
> ***- Blaise Pascal ("Lettres Provinciales", 1657)***

Which loosely translates to

> "If I Had More Time, I Would Have Written a Shorter Letter"

In fact, the amount of things and work I have thrown away greatly outweighs what now exists. I believe that POET and PEAF have achieved elegance and simplicity to some degree but, of course, "we don't live in a perfect world" (as so many Managers I have worked for in the past have reminded me on so many occasions) and there is always more work to do. POET and PEAF will evolve, as everything must do, but for now, it is good enough.

With the benefit of time to think of a suitable response to those Managers, my response now would be:

> "We don't live in a perfect world?
>
> I know - Believe me I know!
>
> If we did, we wouldn't be having this conversation ;-)"

What Was Used to Create Them?

Basically, common sense. It has always amazed me, how many things in business (and in life) do not seem to adhere to any common sense at all, which probably explains why a lot of things that are created to help people improve or mature something, contain a lot of common sense. In addition I have a brain split into two parts (Architecture and Engineering) that work together but also conflict a lot of the time. But it is from this conflict that progress lies.

Methods

- Architecture, Engineering, Logic.

Artefacts

- Input - Air, Water, Nespresso, Earl Grey, Toast, Ham Eggs & Chips, Bombay Sapphire (Tonic), Johnny Walker Black Label (Coke Zero), Whiskers, Paper, Ink, Blood, Sweat, Tears.
- Output - PF2 Book, POET Book, PEAF Book, Pragmatic365.org Website

Guidance

- Common Sense, W.E. Deming, J. Zachman, T. Graves.

Items

- Biological Technology - Kevin - Generally all of him, but mostly his brain, eyes and hands. (His stomach, colon and bladder put in an appearance occasionally, with his posterior providing a supporting role :-), Murphy the cat.
- Mechanical Technology - 25 Buttermere, Braintree, Essex, CM77 7UY, UK, Desk, Chair, Whiteboard (Pens and Eraser).
- Electrical - Challenge Fan Heater, Creative GigaWorks T40 Series II 2.0 PC Speakers
- Information Technology
    - Hardware - Dell Latitude E6520 (Intel i7-2760QM @ 2.4GHz, 8GB RAM), 2 * 32in 2560x1600 LED Monitors, 2 * 24in 1920x1200 LED Monitors, HP Officejet Pro X576, Samsung Galaxy Note 8.
    - Software - MS Windows 10, MS Visio, MS Word, MS Excel, MS PowerPoint, Paint.NET, Integromat, CognitoForms
    - Languages – VBA, VBscript, Javascript, SQL, ASP, HTML, CSS
    - Data – (mp3) David Bowie, Pet Shop Boys, Dean Martin, Chris Rea.

Culture

- God, Honesty, Integrity, Pragmatism, Altruism, Persistence, Passion, Psychology

KEYPOINT:

Use POET and PEAF to make sure you don't make the mistakes that cause 90% of all EA initiatives to fail.

Questions to Ponder

- Do you think that observing failure is a good way to figure out how to improve things?
- What failures have you witnessed in the past?
- What does that tell you about how to improve it?

- **Kevin Lee Smith**
- **40 Years in all phases of Enterprise Transformation**
- **MBTI: (INTJ) Mastermind, (INTP) Architect**
- **DISC: (7414) Result-Oriented**
- **Belbin: Plant, Shaper**

Who Created The Pragmatic Family of Frameworks (PF2)?

A simple man.

My career began at the age of 16 in 1978 as an Electrical and Electronic Apprentice with Marconi Radar Systems (Blackbird Road, Leicester, UK) At that time I was really into electronics and had been playing with little circuits for a few years. It was really exciting. I spent my time between college and "The Factory" where I got the chance to work in many different departments. It was really exciting. Around 1980 I ended up in a Department (New Parks, Leicester UK) called TEPIGEN (**TE**levision **PI**cture **GEN**erator) who had built the visual system for a ship simulator. Six million Pounds of custom built hardware (that had less processing power than the CPU in the phone that's in your pocket) consisting mainly of four racks of "Picture Processors" (Motorola 68000s) driven by a PDP11. It was really exciting. The output was on three channels each delivering 40 degrees field of view which drove three large Barco projectors. Interestingly at one point there were black speckles that kept appearing on the displays, moving about in random patterns and appearing and disappearing in the same apparently random fashion. After months of software and hardware investigation the problem was identified. It was a test Radar across the apron from where our Portacabins where located that was spraying us periodically with microwaves! It was really exciting.

I began my time there hand entering the data which described the terrain and buildings and which fed the picture processors, and wrote my first program in DEC BASIC. Over the next four years or so my programming skills grew, and I moved from BASIC to FORTRAN and then to PASCAL. It was really exciting. The ship simulator turned into a flight simulator which meant it was the biggest video game in the world. It was really exciting. So much so that I would work late into the night (sometimes 48 hours at a stretch) and go into work on Saturdays or Sundays. Right from the beginning it wasn't so much the code I wrote that I got excited about it was more HOW I wrote the code that interested me. I would often spend hours writing a program and finally get it working, only to tear it to pieces and rewrite it in a new and elegant way, often with more features, less code and more opportunity to reuse things later. It was really exciting. Even at that time I spent more time throwing things away than I spent creating things. I believe this is where progress comes from. Sounds totally counter-intuitive I know, but most things of value are counter-intuitive!

Around 1986 the plug was pulled on TEPIGEN and I moved to another department (Fleet, Hampshire, UK) who produced a system called TELEVIEW (an improvement on Teletext and a forerunner of "The Web") for Singapore's Telecom Company (SingTel). I had moved on to C as a programming language. The most elegant and powerful language I have ever used. It took me a while to understand it but after reading the perfect "The C Programming Language" (Kernighan and Ritchie) the penny dropped. It was really exciting.

A brief spell at SD Scicon (1989-1991) was followed by three years working for Deutsche Bank (Singapore) where I found the best food in the world and where my architectural tendencies came to the fore. It was really exciting. While there I created and sold a numerical analysis package for lottery numbers called Mega4D. Returning in 1994 I spent six years working for Eurobase Systems (Chelmsford, UK) doing Application Architecture and creating Architectural and programming frameworks.

From 2000 to 2011 I spent my time working for various Enterprises as a contractor. While interesting, it wasn't very exciting, but all the time, whatever domain I worked in I was always interested in improving it. Each time this met a limit and the limit was always as a consequence of things being done less than effectively and less than efficiently in the preceding step. Hence my roles moved from Application Architecture, Data Architecture and Technology Architecture into Technical Architecture (a bit of a misnomer!) then Solution Architecture then Enterprise Architecture and finally the entire Transformation domain.

Since 2011 I have devoted my time to **Pragmatic**. It is really exciting.

Whilst I have never been an academic person, and never went to university (I have always preferred to "go out and do stuff") I have recognised over the last year that Psychology plays such a vital role in Enterprise Transformation (for good or bad) and so in February 2014 I began a BSc (Honours) Psychology degree with The Open University. It is really exciting.

MBTI

My MBTI is a split between **INTJ** and **INTP.**

INTJ - Sometimes referred to as the "Architect," or the "Strategist," people with INTJ personalities are highly analytical, creative and logical.

Strengths: Enjoys theoretical and abstract concepts. High expectations. Good at listening. Takes criticism well. Self-confident and hard-working.

Weaknesses: Can be overly analytical and judgmental. Very perfectionistic. Dislikes talking about emotions. Sometimes seems callous or insensitive.

INTP - People who score as INTP are often described as quiet and analytical. They enjoy spending time alone, thinking about how things work and coming up with solutions to problems. INTPs have a rich inner world and would rather focus their attention on their internal thoughts rather than the external world. They typically do not have a wide social circle, but they do tend to be close to a select group of people.

Strengths: Logical and objective. Abstract thinker. Independent. Loyal and affectionate with loved ones.

Weaknesses: Difficult to get to know. Can be insensitive. Prone to self-doubt. Struggles to follow rules. Has trouble expressing feelings.

DISC

My DISC Profile is 7414 and categorised as **Result-Oriented.**

Result-Oriented people display self-confidence, which some may interpret as arrogance. They actively seek opportunities that test and develop their abilities to accomplish results. Result-Oriented persons like difficult tasks, competitive situations, unique assignments, and "important" positions. They undertake responsibilities with an air of self-importance and display self-satisfaction once they have finished.

Result-Oriented people tend to avoid constraining factors such as direct controls, time-consuming details, and routine work. Because they are forceful and direct, they may have difficulties with others. Result-Oriented people prize their independence and may become restless where involved with group activities or committee work. Although Result-Oriented people generally prefer to work alone, they may persuade others to support their efforts especially when completing routine activities.

Result-Oriented people are quick-thinkers, and they are impatient and fault-finding with those who are not They evaluate others on their ability to get results. Result Oriented people are determined and persistent even in the face of antagonism. They take command of the situation when necessary, whether or not they are in charge. In their uncompromising drive for results, they may appear blunt and uncaring.

Belbin

Belbin categorises me as a **Plant** (Creative and inventive individuals, Plants are the ones in the team most likely to come up with new ideas and suggestions. The name comes from Dr Belbin's original research. It was discovered that there was no initial spark of an idea in a team unless a creative person was "planted" in each team) and a **Shaper** (Shapers are people who challenge the team to improve. They are dynamic and usually extroverted people who enjoy stimulating others, questioning norms, and finding the best approaches for solving problems.).

Putting MBTI, DISC and Belbin together just about sums me up to a tee.

Different people have different profiles, and different profiles fit into different roles in different ways. We all kind of know this but do we ever take it into account?

> KEYPOINT:
>
> Use people for the type of person they are, not the type of person you want them to be. If we were all the same, nothing would ever get done.

Questions to Ponder

- What are the MBTI, DISC and Belbin profiles of the people in your Enterprise?
- Do they all suit their roles?
- Have you ever found someone to be a "difficult person" or a "loose cannon"?
- If so, did their MBTI/DISC/Belbin profile taken into account?

PF2 introduces the Companies and Frameworks that are part of the Pragmatic Family.

The Introduction section of PF2 introduces the companies that are part of the Pragmatic Family.

Pragmatic 365 is a non-profit research company. Pragmatic EC is a consulting company.

Most consultancies only want to sell you fish.

Pragmatic will teach you how to fish.

Use Pragmatic Frameworks (for free) to improve your Enterprise.

PEAF Certified training, provides everything to enable you to adopt PEAF.

PEAF Focused Workshops, allow you to focus on specific areas.

Access to the Pragmatic Publishing Platform is granted by graduating from an Instructor led course.

P3 allows Enterprises to easily produce and maintain their own Frameworks and publish them to books, their intranet and mobile devices.

P3 is a component based authoring system.

The Language section of PEFF introduces fundamental terminology that is used throughout Pragmatic's Frameworks.

Be ever vigilant of the hidden confusion that language can create.

Everything is a System.

The Word Enterprise does not mean "large" or "large IT" or "senior". It is a general noun.

There is no hidden connotation to Pragmatic's use of the word "Transformation".

A Framework is an expression of Best Practice comprising information in at least one area (Methods, Artefacts, Guidance, Items, Culture) and optionally information regarding its Adoption.

Theory is just as important as Practice

Colour

=

Information

=

Understanding.

The Culture section of POET defines the roles and the culture required.

Someone should be Accountable for the strategically important Transformation capability of the Enterprise.

"Culture Trumps Everything"

-Kevin Smith

"Culture is like the speed of light.

Very difficult to change."

- Kevin Lee Smith

Bad Culture knows no bounds.

It can destroy lives.

And Enterprises.

Good Culture knows no bounds.

It can lift lives.

And Enterprises.

The human brain is easily fooled.

True value is not measured by the numbers of Clicks or Likes.

Sometimes the best course of action is to not do what you are being told to do.

Short term gratification (quick wins) most often leads to long term failure. Delaying short term gratification, most often leads to long term success.

Don't be swayed by the majority. They are wrong 80% of the time!

"I hope our wisdom will grow with our power, and teach us, that the less we use our power the greater it will be."

- Thomas Jefferson.

"Nobody cares how much you know, until they know how much you care".

- Theodore Roosevelt

"It's hard to see a halo when you're looking for horns."

- Cullen Hightower

"How often it is that the angry man rages denial, of what his inner self is telling him."
- Frank Herbert (Dune)

Those who are Unconsciously Incompetent, are the one's most passionate that they are right!

Success should not be promoted.

Do not let the past, unduly affect the future.

Competence grows linearly.

Incompetence grows exponentially.

"The trouble with Sociopaths, is that they are very, very nice people!"

- Kevin Lee Smith

People with different personality traits are required for different roles

"In all chaos, there is a cosmos. In all disorder, a secret order."

- Carl Jung

Architecture and Engineering are two sides of the same coin.

Think (and Plan) Strategically (Architecture), Act Tactically (Engineering)..

The line between Architecture and Engineering is a blurred one.

Architecture is performed largely in the early phases of Transformation, while Engineering is performed largely in the later phases.

Architecture and Engineering can be performed within any phase.

The relationship between Architecture and Engineering as we move from the top to the bottom phases is complex.

Know and exploit the fundamental difference between Architects and Engineers.

Architecture and Engineering, bring important things to the table, and makes the whole much more than the sum of its parts.

A happy productive person, balances what they are good at, with what they love, what others need, and what they want.

"The secret of business is to know something that nobody else knows."
- Aristotle Onassis

"Every noble work is at first, impossible."
- Thomas Carlyle

"Architecture provides the Landing strip of intent, for any viable implementation to land on."
- {{Gareth Llewellyn}}

"The value of Architecture is intangible.
If it were tangible, it would be Engineering."
- Kevin Lee Smith

The Pragmatic Architects Creed™ sorts the wheat from the chaff.

For each phase of the Transformation cascade, people speak either a different dialect or language from the phases above and below.

Solution Architecture is too important to be owned by Projects.

Recognise that there are two types of EA: 1. Those that improve how EA is done. 2. Those that "do" EA (Strategic Transformation Planning and Governance).

Type 1 Enterprise Architects help an Enterprise to increase their EA maturity.

Type 1 Enterprise Architect's work, is primarily to; 1) Evangelise the benefits of EA. 2) Support the internal EA Team to mature how EA is performed.

Type 2 Enterprise Architects do Strategic Transformation planning.

Type 2 Enterprise Architect's work, is primarily to; 1) support Strategising. 2) perform Roadmapping 3) Govern executing projects.

While "firefighters" are always necessary, more resources need to be brought to bear as "fire prevention officers".

You cannot change what you don't understand and you cannot understand what you cannot see.

HOW each part of your Enterprise does what they do, shows the real contribution toward achieving the Enterprises Mission.

IT is special not because it is IT, but because IT tends to be responsible for a large part of HOW an Enterprise does what it does.

Recognise and deal with the fact that IT and The Business do constitute "Two Tribes".

IT should never say "No" to the Business. It should say "Yes, but...".

You cannot change what you don't understand and you cannot understand what you cannot see.

PEAF refers to various roles, most of which will already exist in an Enterprise.

An SIB with allocated budget and power is mandatory for Governance & Lobbying to operate effectively.

An EASG with delegated budget and power is mandatory for Governance & Lobbying to operate effectively.

The Appendix section contains information on the background of PF2, POET, PEAF and the author.

Use POET and PEAF to make sure you don't make the mistakes that cause 90% of all EA initiatives to fail.

Use people for the type of person they are, not the type of person you want them to be. If we were all the same, nothing would ever get done.

All Pragmatic books contain a Keypoint section.

www.Pragmatic365.org is the official source for all PF2/POET/PEAF related materials, and is constantly evolving.

Pragmatic EA is a non-profit research company, dedicated to developing Best Practice in relation to the structure and transformation of Enterprises.

Sources

- Book cover: Tropical Storm Lee - NASA/NOAA GOES Project Science Team.
- Stereogram used on "Hitting the Wall" produced by Easy Stereogram Builder - www.easystereogrambuilder.com
- "Brain Function with gears and cogs" used on the "Slaves to Psychology" graphic from BigStock - www.bigstockphoto.com/search/digitalista
- Technical Debt - www.wikipedia.org/wiki/Technical_debt
- Zachman Framework - www.wikipedia.org/wiki/Zachman_Framework
- TOGAF (The Open Group Architecture Framework) - www.opengroup.org/togaf/
- Business Motivation Model - www.omg.org/spec/BMM/
- Enhanced Business Motivation Model - www.MotivationModel.com
- ITIL (IT Infrastructure Library) - www.itil-officialsite.com
- COBIT (Control Objectives for Information and Related Technology) - www.wikipedia.org/wiki/Cobit

Resources

- www.Pragmatic365.org is the official source for all **Pragmatic** related materials.

Here is listed various sources and references to things referred to in the **Pragmatic** Frameworks.

You can always access the most up to date material online at www.Pragmatic365.org.

KEYPOINT:

www.Pragmatic365.org is the official source for all PF2/POET/PEAF related materials, and is constantly evolving.

Pragmatic 365

CONNECTING THE DOTS

KEYPOINT:

Pragmatic EA is a non-profit research company, dedicated to developing Best Practice in relation to the structure and transformation of Enterprises.

www.ingramcontent.com/pod-product-compliance
Ingram Content Group UK Ltd.
Pitfield, Milton Keynes, MK11 3LW, UK
UKHW052002041026
15590UKWH00008B/2105

9 781908 42459